SELECTED POEMS

REVISED & NEW

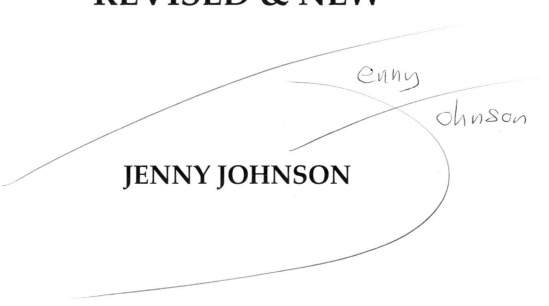

JENNY JOHNSON

First published in 2013
by
Brimstone Press Ltd.
The Mount
Buckhorn Weston
SP8 5HT

www.brimstonepress.co.uk

Printed and bound by CPI Group (UK) Ltd, Croydon, CR0 4YY

ISBN 978-1-906385-40-8

For Marilyn, Karen, Jessie and Sam

ACKNOWLEDGEMENTS

Most of these poems have been published in my collections: *The Wisdom Tree: Poems 1975 to 93* (University of Salzburg) and *Neptune's Daughters* (Expansions Unlimited, Nottingham). Previously uncollected poems have appeared in *GreenSpirit* and *Sarasvati*.

I wish to thank all those family members, friends and teachers who have encouraged me to write, especially the poet Fred Beake – who championed my work when others chose to ignore it.

I am grateful to Roger Grainger – actor, dramatherapist and versatile writer – for providing the Foreword. Also, I thank Naa Ahinee Mensah for her wonderful cover design – she is a Ghanaian artist, living in Nottingham. You might like to visit their websites – www.rogergrainger.co.uk and www.ahineemensah.co.uk – for further information.

GRAY OR GREY?

I always spell the word *gray* that way because, to me, it suits the colour it describes better than when it is spelt with an *e* in the middle. Perhaps because I am half American by birth, I prefer the American way of writing it – which is also an earlier English way!

THE ORDER OF THE POEMS

I have deliberately put the single poems in alphabetical order – except where the first word of a title is either the definite or indefinite article – so that they can be found easily. I did consider placing them in chronological order, but decided against this: my development as a poet has not always been a linear one!

FOREWORD

For Marianne, whom Jenny Johnson writes about in one of her poems, death is "the crony in the valley". Unlike the author, we have never met or even seen Marianne, yet the phrase hits us in the eye, as we remember what we have not seen, and will never now forget. Johnson opens this kind of door in our minds. Often, poems look as though they are describing a place, a happening, a group or a person, which the poet is re-experiencing and now records for us: something neither dramatic nor obviously important, we might think, particularly as we don't happen to know the context – which is why it is so amazing to find ourselves actually part of it.... Poetry like this is its own background. Hold my hand and shut up, it says.

How it does so is what poetry itself is about, presented here in the clearest of ways. Poetry is not only the way in but also the richness found there. Telling us to keep our distance, it takes us to its heart. We find ourselves both ordinary and transformed. The raw material of Johnson's work is the lingua franca of all poetry: the transformed ordinary. Despite the alphabetical, non-chronological order in this book, we can tell which is her earlier work by the way it strikes home with contrasts that are strange and familiar, poem after poem shocking us out of the security of our expectation. The struggle between thought and feeling strives for containment by a paring down of emotions as far as that richness at the centre – a cutting down to the quick, the exposed nerve. The impression left is of an experience so intense that words are forced from their habit of prevarication and used to show us what the thing itself really was. Was – or is? The memory-picture knocks, and the words are quarried to give it immediacy.

In Johnson's early poems, the skill of quarrying stands out more distinctly than in later work. This is because the recollected emotion is still so powerfully present: the impact of the sequences *Rise and Fall* and *A Year of Dreams* is of an astounding lucidity, the analysis of pains and joys that refuses the indulgence of inviting sympathy. This relates to an early period of Johnson's life when poetry was the discipline bringing relief to extreme emotional pain. Nevertheless, it would be misguided to spend time searching for autobiographical clues in work whose outstanding characteristic is an ability simply to be itself. Her insight into others' suffering is evident in the depth of understanding that is intrinsic to all her poetry. These earlier poems have a particularly moving force for this reader, perhaps because of the stoicism I find in them.

Later on in Johnson's writing, there is a change, a further deepening. In *Neptune's Daughters*, she tells us that

"The heart cannot be honed like thought:
lessons are learned without timetables, indices."

This poetry reveals a quality that was always there, but now shows more plainly – a natural profundity I associate with a letting go of tensions. As early as *Poets* – written just after the sequence *A Year of Dreams* – Johnson describes the creativity of those who relent:

"their words make whole;
and somewhere within our abysses, they build us
a listening room."

It is out of the tension between reticence and disclosure that poetry springs. Where it does so, however, is neither in the past nor the future, but within the present. In *Pitlochry*, it is here and now that "sun-lofts are found for feelings long buried."

A Way of Living sets the tone for much later writing:

"This is the home of Caroline, and Hermione.
Mid-January has come: in its afternoon tints of
sepia and copper ... "

It is the poetry of the rescued moment, stopping the world just long enough for us to take in what it is that we are really looking at. This is the gift that Wordsworth had, when he chose to use it. Here, it is employed with sensitivity and skill: poets have an instinctive knowledge of the depth that lies hidden in the commonplace – once their own ordernariness has been exorcised. Only then, as Johnson writes in *The Wisdom Tree*, are they fully aware that there are "enough jewels for the journey".

If there is a single poem in this book that enshrines the meaning of them all, it is the one called *Allowing It To Loosen*. Here is the first stanza:

"Not consciously, quickly
releasing the hurt of it,
but allowing it times
for loosening in secret....
That is the key."

If, by some unfortunate chance, you can only read one poem in this unforgettable collection, let it be this.

ROGER GRAINGER
February, 2013

CONTENTS

RISE AND FALL

A YEAR OF DREAMS

AFTER THE TERIYAKI

After the teriyaki – the trampoline.
Eleven is lean; ravenous.
In the in-between time before sunset,
before the onset of puberty,
he becomes the Man-Boy;
the defender of his Mother –
Mother who is creative with her courage.

His father is irregularly absent.

The cat, Sky, curls its blackness
into his heart.
Nana is witness to it –
to his suppleness with words,
to his innocence tinged with dark.
She is fearful of asymmetry.

Eleven is lean; ravenous:
Fifteen has a talent for design.
As an only sister, she becomes
the storm's eye: his balance:
his compass.

ALL HALLOWS

All Hallows light, brittle between highest, south clouds,
feels essence most when shell becomes fractured:
an essence which seems sucked in, seems blown out –
– beyond any orbit.

Indoors – eyes clasp the clover pink vaporiser;
in the shade, heart-shaped holes in its sides
provide lights for giants – patterns for the plain wall:

behind the scalloped circle of the main window,
candle flame constantly wavers …

ALLOWING IT TO LOOSEN

Not consciously, quickly
releasing the hurt of it,
but allowing it times
for loosening in secret....
That is the key.

For seventeen years,
my namesake was a close friend.
In the end, when she sliced me from her prime,
I became too ungrounded for grief.

Now, as my strength rises,
I strive less.
Recurring dreams of the namesake
remind me to *wait, wait*
for my heart to unbind its hurt.

ANCIENT AND MODERN

To our surprise it was in the close that we halted –
where ancient stone was clean;
where stained glass doors were modern, yet not incongruous.

At the west entrance we were offered vestments –
relics of cotton, silk, broderie anglaise;
were given brass-rubbings and quaint drawings of misericords;
were shown nothing that was too plain, too decorative.

Afterwards, on the outskirts of the city –
away from the herbs and resins of the refectory –
our established warder, Turner, prepared strong beverages;
and punctually attended to numbers; uniforms; luggage.

When the emptied coach promptly departed,
the cups in our palms became curiously heavy.

ANIMUS

Born in the wake of war,
I was wholly unaware of my naval father
glorying in America.

Pennilessly hiding in a West Country port,
my mother did not dare to flaunt her flag.
Her Jewish blood had bubbled, had re-cooled

by the time she launched me....
My adopters provided a lockable berth,
the wife steering the husband:

who was water watcher, boat investor,
who would perch upon banks, bridges, edges of shores.
How often I searched in his face for some hint of alternatives!

I have searched in the faces and arms of a number of men
for that one who pulled away – perhaps without weeping.
I remember the birth of my child: how the shock wave came

like a sob – because of that maleness.
And I glance at him now, attempting not to accuse:
glance at his eyes; which command, and are strange.

ANOREXIA

Only when she had flown a thousand miles
to the south – had chosen to halt by untitled,
midsummer sea – could she eat.

She returned there often – always alone; bane-free:
from the hill, she could feel how a wave gave zest
to her premature heart.

Till one day, on withdrawing into her pastel frame,
she caught herself turning northeast – to the Advent light:
caught mauves on her apple boughs.

Now, despite her unseasonable fasts, she discerned
strength in the falling away of late summer, late autumn:
at last, she learned about the feasts of the heart.

Newest moons of apple, pear, were appearing on her plate....
Re-entering the orchard, she began tasting them.

ART DECO, MIAMI BEACH

The New Year translucency remains within sea:
art deco turquoise.
The sky looks full of itself, with its
frequent metallic fowl.
Underneath it, young men lounge on chaises longues –
salt-clean; keen for uniformity.
Everywhere, there are pastels of purple, coral, jade.

The foreignness of Florida is stronger than that of
Italy, Germany: the language of English conceals
parallel rather than linked worlds.
People have an air of detachment:
a vocabulary of charm.

As I walk along the pearly beach,
my mood shifts: I begin depressed by the
absence of cliffs – of vitality in
tides and condominiums.
The rhythm in my hip – the afternoon light
laced with a wakening wind – pull me to the pier:
to the pelican's poised beak and wing.

In a while – willing to connect – I focus on detail:
the Beth Jacob Synagogue; the Wolfsonian Museum.
As six o'clock darkness falls, oceanfront hotels
line their aprons with premature loudness.
Puerto Ricans, Cubans, have opened bikini-thin shops.
At South Pointe, by a fitness circuit,
the elderly, orthodox Jews whisper.

The art of imitation – imitation of art? –
is as constant as in ancient Rome.
Americans pay homage to it in limousines –
or on roller blades.

AUNT SUNNY

Jessica Sunderland –
known to the annual visiting children as Aunt Sunny –
detached her green baize curtain from her terrace house door.

Revealing practised, freckled forearms,
she placed starched cotton on mahogany,
and wheeled in a trolley full of doily-covered, willow-patterned platters.

To earn such delicacies as glacé cherries and clotted cream,
the children recited Kipling and Masefield on a garden dais;
while beyond untouchable fences, there passed phlegmatic engines....

Yet only a few years later,
the widowed aunt would be no more significant than faint, faint doubt.

BACHELOR

Alfred Newland Johnson, bachelor, of Leighton
Buzzard, Bedfordshire: I remember his baldness, caries,
irresolute moustache; his intermittent, nervous cough;
the frequent "don't you know", in the middle of his monologues;
and his eyes, pale from reading.

With two brothers curbed by the First World War, and a third
turning mechanic, he was the sole intellectual of his family....
Formerly a Bluecoat boy, he became a private
tutor in classics and mathematics. Christening me Jennifer
Jo – he told me of games called equations and alphabets.

I remember his mother, the Bedfordshire house: the ritual
removal of teeth before meals, the mangle in the garden,
the railway pulling on to the road; postmistress Dora;
cousin Esther, juggling with Cox's and Bramley's;
Jessica, holding her bowl of cherries.

He had travelled worlds – had chosen to absorb nothing:
everything! I remember the egg-soft optimism in his voice;
the ten-shilling note that he never forgot for my birthday:
and that habit of being surprised – and half lost.

BARRIERS

She stands in the allowance queue absorbed in her Kafka;
pregnant; unaccommodated.
Everything about her is conspicuously pallid:
the khaki coat; the sallow finger;
the anti-hysteria face.

In their nourished house,
her brigadier father and her satellite mother
are engrossed in so much guilt, so much self-pity
that they grow exhausted –
and forget to unbar the door.

The queue for benefits jerkily shifts.
The foetus – a future mediator perhaps –
turns without warning in his wet elastic habitat.
The girl ceases reading –
and is not unaware of involuntary softenings.

BEECH OWL BARN

They sleep downstairs, close to their Cornish earth –
a granite-mason, his wife and child.

Upstairs, above the birthing room, a balcony faces
land safe as lambs;
and looks into the garden, where the Buddha, the standing stones –
even the disused telephone kiosk – accept their places.

The husband is filling the belly of the barn
with his own creations:
at one with woody grains and tones, he understands
how to implant his vision there; and when to reveal it.

His wife cuts their saffron cake, pours jasmine tea;
like her husband, she remembers beyond time,
beyond imperfection –
where sleeping and rebirthing are unnecessary.

Here, they have learned how standing stones may sometimes
form an ellipse, rather than a pure circle:
how a sapling, enclosed and guarded by this granite,
may be off-centre.

Their little daughter, recalling still more, knows
that all is well.

THE BELL-FLY

In their prelude to transformation, humbug-coloured insects
droned around Fern – who, kneeling alone, had suddenly grown
staccato fear-of-stings.

Yet, just as they were about to close in,
the drones changed into white, bell-shaped flowers –
frangible as butterflies; relinquishing, one by one,
percussion of shells.

At the right time, Tam appeared – with a
mute blue cloth in his hand; he beckoned to Fern:
side by side, they cleansed the bestrewn floor.

Meanwhile, the bell-flowers had formed themselves
into bracelets, necklaces, coronets – which Tam and Fern
spontaneously wore …

till, filled with a lightness of song within these charms,
they found how, in one moment, they could
float upwards; could drift through highest windows.

Below them – the town, the forest, had lifted their mists
to acknowledge first light.

BETWEEN THEMSELVES

There were usually two characters:
she played them not only alone in lanes and railway
compartments, but also on the beach – unconsciously avoiding
its limpet-points. Crowds were not common here.

Sometimes, they conversed in the company of total unknowns....
Often they mentioned a third, a fourth person:
families were involved: euphonious names began
falling through the air like down.

Now and again, they were overheard in a café,
mellowing their tones – aiding the digestion of shallow-cupped
desserts....

And if Mother was there...? She seldom attempted to comment,
even to one of her Celtic friends – even to a
voice that was keenly kind.

BORDERLAND

Ascending towards midsummer,
with evening clouds over the river Otter –
over the curve of incoming tides –
I am drawn to the border of newborn consciousness.

These wildfowl are stilled: they are held within reflections of
taming sunlight. High on my right,
a helix of lark song begins....
Whichever way I turn, there are mellowing headlands.

In Sidmouth, I am nourished by straight rain;
by the cerise-browns of Devon sandstone.
Challenged further west, I run along the damp shore
in luminous boots.

The estuary beach feels abandoned
except for the gull and the shell –
and a current of expectancy
out there ... in here.

But now, where do I go...?
The essence of the place calls out: "Today, you have sampled:
tomorrow, you travel inland:
here, on the very edge, you may play ... play."

Suddenly, a child leaps high by the fringes of the water.
I dance alongside: I become White Wave….
Always, we are close to an unseen guardian, she and I:
in the sorrow-joy; the sea-sky.

BREAKING FREE

Wherever she treads on those fringes of town
that encompass her fear – there, it comes upon her;
and there: a mean, green shed;
gray-roofed; opaque-windowed;
its doors semi-ajar – like trappers' arms.

Then, it is in her backyard: hard by the
washing line, the play square, the kitchen.
And then, it becomes the bedroom:
the narrowing, gray-green walls
pinching the dregs of childhood.

Whenever she hears his drunken steps on the stair –
fear plunges her into a numbness....
She attempts to scream at her lockless door –
but the larynx goes cold....

Sick Mother lives on pilules and elixirs;
is enclosed in a world of sorrows kept hot;
of simmering denial.
Such helplessness binds her daughter as fast as
Father's abuse. Night after night, she etches
"Liar! Guilty!" on the bruised heart....

Just once, looking in the glass, the girl acknowledges her
pair of wigs – blond basins trapping her
spring of hair: which she imagines
long as a wand, full as a curtain;
free …
freer than a mountain wind.

THE BRIDGE

A month or two after his fifty-first birthday,
James was taken to the bridge.

The therapist ordered her twenty-eight patients
to keep to the left; to walk in pairs, sedately;
to watch collectively the orange foliage.

James disobeyed: he stepped on to the opposing footpath;
stopped before the advice for intending suicides.

Scared of neither depth nor height,
he stared at the decreasing obscurity of the river:

it was forty years since he had sensed this bridge,
since he had found on the other side his twin brother;
disinfected; one-eyed; unacceptably dead.

The therapist purposely failed to notice
his need to communicate, to comprehend.

The unbiased westerly wind simply anaesthetised.

BURNT SIENNA BLUES

In an area known as the Colony – reclaimed marshland –
in the coffin-shaped middle room of a converted flat, a girl
curls; listens to northern radio:

forgets the French windows facing the blanched
wall; the Welsh dresser; the green peeling of
paper – not old enough to hold arsenic;

the burnt sienna carpet stained from years of sour-sweet
babies. It is summer. Very hot. The electric light is
permanently on.

In one of the neighbouring rooms – tinctures of sky are
confined to a casement.... A little beneath it a cot-child
continually pains; pains: quite hospital-pale.

A drain smells – yet is steadier than a moist ceiling;
than February bedbugs. A rumour of fish and chips
fills the hall....

Someone calls for the mother upstairs; a telephone
rings behind locked partitions. When her child is well,
the girl will slip on her turquoise bikini and wheel him

**to the estuary: to watch those diaper white yachts; that cargo
leaving for Norway; the sun – cooling on a violet
tide; on a mushroom-coloured sand.**

THE CAPTIVE

On the ninth day, nine terrorists came:
they bound him, within a pear-shaped cave;
they closed up the aperture....
They left him a half-loaf –
left him the fluid from the rough, sunless roof.

At the turning of the tide, the captive awakened:
pains crawled all over him like ants.
But he refused to be ill with hostility....
He loosed himself; he inched forward –
yearning for the leniency of light.

Desperation lent him slow strength;
and on the eleventh day, he emerged from his limestone tomb –
shaken, bruised, willing to be taken
by anyone with a kind arm, and a quiet eye.

Though nobody was there in the astringent air –
nobody....
The vibrations were too sudden.
The sea commanded, "Come to *me*! Come!"

He almost preferred the enclosed, the learnt,
to this demanding, vast brightness:
he was released – and yet still fastened.

CATHARSIS

When gusty rain finally arrived,
Penelope, who had felt too quiet in the stout house,
was seen by no one running between twilight trees,
with her autumn hair loosened,
and her eyes focused on rhythmic distance.

She was not entirely uncultured in the children's home;
but the wilderness had grown too strong since mother had left –
mother-who-could-not-be-recalled.

That concentrated anger of tidal water,
that diagonal wet cut of blind wind on hand,
startled till the knuckles were bloodless.

She stood penitentially yet indulgently,
while the forces around her increased, and absorbed,
while the wilderness within diminished;
and wondered whether mother-who-could-not-be-recalled
was familiar with this: the receiving-before-the-giving.

CHINESE ANGELICA

Angelica sinensis, my herb-sister,
the sister of ginseng:
your root floats in my tumbler of water –
its fragrance an arch between savoury and sweet.

As soon as I have opened – you begin
your balancing act on my first three bodies:
physical; emotional; mental.

You become – refiner of the contours;
my chromium strengthener:
become – nurse of the creased moods;
my gardener of thoughts.

Afterwards, resting on my bed – I feel like I do
in my Indian cotton: am shaped like a
vase; like a frond within that vase.

We are daily inseparable, you and I;
your vibrations are subtler than mine:
you continuously heal....
We are just two of many.

CHIROPODY

On the third Thursday of each month,
Alice boards the green bus:
her daughter Hilary makes for the upper deck.
They journey across the Downs to the Black Boy,
Whiteladies Road, the Victoria Rooms.

In the Clifton waiting room, Hilary stares at the ceiling –
the cornices, the roses – while her mother, behind shining
doors, anticipates treatment. The chiropodist smiles
through strong lenses, his hair profuse on his forehead.

Later, they visit a house with homemade fruit sweets
in the window. And on their return, Roland, the husband,
massages Alice's stockinged feet with uncomplicated
warm hands....
It is nineteen fifty....

Hilary watches, hypnotised. These feet are as pampered
as the dogs, the rich leather of each lace-up
shaped specially for deformity. Those shins are too thin
for that big-boned frame: the ankles are frequently sprained,
crêpe-bound. Occasionally – when weakened eyes misjudge
boiling water – a toe joint, an instep, is gingerly
anointed with copper-and-gold.

THE CHOICE

Stone-like, within a thin tower,
she looks through barred windows at summer's communities
toiling, dancing, settling about her.

The tower house is so mean that they believe it to be empty;
until a brave stranger enters her evening –
and releases three decades.

Lantern in hand, he leads her through silvering woods
to a hidden pond – where he bathes her feet.
There is oil for her wounds and wine for her pallor.

Soon there will be further gifts, he tells her:
companionship, fire.
Yet, when dawn comes, she is gone.

He searches the forest, convinced that she has fallen:
not even for a moment does he dream she has chosen to regress –
chosen the limited.

Only the unhurried sun finds her:
it slips from between those bars on to her dark, bowed head –
neither condoning nor condemning.

THE CHROMOSCOPE

At the first sign of the moon, I come to the
hillside chromoscope; the hexagonal crystal;
the healing shrine.

Here are six windows, each containing the
same six stones: one for each colour of the
rainbow – apart from violet, which illuminates the roof.

Attendants in saffron robes and caps direct me
to a central fountain, a mountain spring:
spanning it, is a translucent, movable platform –
– supported by delicate quartz.

Turning to a window which is neither too bright nor too dim,
I receive its wavelengths, one by one:
to each colour, there belongs a distinct sound.

To the ground of my becoming, flows red depth of garnet;
to my womb and my gut – orange of carnelian;
to my solar plexus – citrine yellow.

To my half-opened heart, flows aventurine green;
to my half-loosened throat – azurite blue;
to my brow – indigo of lapis;
to my crown – amethyst violet....

The hardest task is to absorb the yellow: fright at its
directness rises from my diaphragm, and tightens in my throat;
and on my brow.

Eventual release begins with the rays of
azurite and lapis; and ends in a
cycle of yawns; weeping; laughter.

CLINIC

In a building that will not easily tell its name,
they falter around a stale pastel of wall –
divided from each other by more than a tiled vinyl.

An alternative door is glossed over, sealed.
A mother smokes. In her tone, in the squint of her
tanned boy, lives a repressed violence.

A social worker comes and goes: the custard
colour of the bandeau in her ginger hair neither
enlivens nor perturbs.... A psychiatrist patterns words.

Through a window, his client glimpses the kiosk for
harlequins – the costumes hanging askew:
is aware of a brief timelessness; a peculiar hunger.

CLOVER

The golden train has carried me down from town to
sea: where rising blue is rinsed with sinking
red – is so warmed by the season that if it were not for my
grave cotton, I should be embraced by it immediately.

Looking behind me – I find once more the town's
square tower: its protectiveness and power – above which
grow those thunderclouds; those cherry clouds of
sunset. No threat exists: there is a wedding of tones.

To the north – the untrodden road coaxes; occasional,
pink-washed houses crouch by rocks; and ancient
shops bear signs that are neither cowardly nor bold.

To the south – hills transcend; I walk towards their
stillness; kneel in the grass to absorb its fragrance of
humility: become conscious of beginnings – and the absence of pain.

As soon as I am touched by the clover, I know that for a moment at
least – there is no need for choice: I can remain here – at a
joining of many, many ways; within the flower of the whole.

COLD COMFORT

When I am febrile, I like pampering myself:
prone on my bed, eyes heavily closed,
I breathe in eucalyptus, wintergreen, peppermint.

Maybe an aeroplane hones overhead; benign;
like a passing pain:
as a child, I anticipated crashes, bombs.

Or the fortic tank makes lukewarm promises;
or the forecast, east wind, not wholly awake,
tells a romantic story through the gas fire.

Infections can release tensions.
Poems come slowly at such times, as if dazed;
images remain undusted: it ceases to matter.

And often, my son takes dusky coins into town,
each of his hands tacky with additives;
his mind quite unconcerned with any future.

COMING OF AGE

Even at the age of four she had known about sky:
how it was more, truly more than a stripe of
blue across the paper-top.

Fourteen years later, high-heeled on the ferry, the hovercraft,
she could concentrate fully on the hand – yearning to draw,
draw: her mind had begun to involve itself in politics;
satire.

The composure of her father, the meekness of her mother –
the familiar languor of Hampshire tongues – influenced her
less mysteriously than her terraced home's
conservatory cat; or contemplative breakfast;
or flowered, flowered lounge.

COMING TO TERMS

It is finished, this going, this coming to terms,
this lifting of the soul from its taciturn soil,
this mould, which has clung to the bone too long.

Yet finished too soon, is the uniform pallor
of nurse and anaesthetist, surgeon and priest:
their authorised prayers in the etherised dust
are left vacant as gloves, aseptic as scalpels.

THE CONTENTIOUS WIFE

She arrives insufferably late.

Her visited husband tenses, reddens, listens:
her companion slackens....

Both of them are conscious of the concentrated hatred –
in her voice, in her eye.

Yet neither man turns violent:
through the willow-laced window comes abundant sweet light.

And then a youngster appears; who swings between the chair arms:
wanting, wanting laughter.

CRESCENT

In her recurring dreams under the newest moon,
she is borne by the lagoon's breath towards
fan tracery on stalwart walls.

Home, as always, is semi-unknown.
She is journeying again through rounded archways;
and again, through a brown and cream labyrinth –

a labyrinth which is expanding according to her needs;
which never confuses....
Infinite freedom, infinite protection, are there.

Coming to a room with a curvaceous dining table,
she rediscovers her cradle of a basket; and her scallops;
and her segments of mandarin, and cantaloupe.

Watching over her, are impressions of mature man,
mature woman – each with prominent eyebrows....
With their permission, she is waiting for the dawn,
the downpour; the resolving, gouache rainbow.

DEADLOCK

It is Lent:
I swallow my dried bread, my decaffeinated coffee;
I lie down, emptiness hissing in my head,
and fractions of curtain shutting out
the hardening light.

How can I meditate when the mind
becomes an abandoned, half-desiccated pond
instead of a fund:
when Alexander –
for whom surfaces and clocks constantly matter –
makes pellets out of surplus energy;
and aims with uncompromising eyes?

DERELICT

Haggard as November, he thirsts for the river.
How fast it winds! –
as though it were cleaning a secret wound
on the hip of the land.

And under the night's untenanted sky,
he listens to the loosened –
to the wind-without-code on the birdless tree,
to the plummeting leaf, with its brief goodbye.

And he listens. And he listens to the chastened, the blanched.

DISCONNECTIONS

Early indoors, the March fog is matched by
tobacco-mist: Antony grows defiant about his
recent cancer; the aggressive shine on his nicotined
hand sets him apart.

Antonia longs to play – to conceal herself: all day,
her cats may walk on the draining board – or even on a
hotplate; her dog may open doors indiscriminately –
greasing the mahogany.

The daughter who lives away remains between them,
unacknowledged. Dust from years of unharnessed rebellion
rests in a zone of paralysis – on the mock-Victorian
chair; by the artificial fire, the Braque print.

Half quirkily, Antonia laughs and hums. Antony
baths – and exits in time for intense employment....
Antonia visits the haunts of the elderly: there,
her expression is always inscrutable – and poems keep inside.

THE DISTURBANCE AT ST ANNE'S

How conspicuously small I seemed within the emptied, Saturday church!
Grandfather Godfrey was playing the organ.
How the sound pained me…!
Surely the silver-and-red stained glass admitted suspect light,
and the knotted wood floor had been polished by a dishonest spirit….

I whined.
Grandfather ceased rehearsing. He turned towards me….
He was benign, yet unable to communicate.

Outside, we paused on exposed, supposedly hallowed ground –
contemplating valley things;
anticipating the sting of spring wind….
Then hand in concerned hand, we descended the hill.
And I longed for the familiar cottage –
for the curative steam and warm towelling of home.

And I fell asleep so tranquilly, so gradually, that night…!
Only in my dreams was I conscious of unevenness.

THE DRYAD

Day after soft green day, she wandered through the forest –
nameless on purpose;
tasting tested fruit;
learning the location of each leaf, each tepid pool.

Sometimes,
she would welcome the sun with her lids quite closed....
The delicate gold, violet, white,
would continuously contract, and expand....

Till one still dawn,
an explorer rode by, ordering:
"Show her the proud prairies; the sky-power."

Yet when his attendants attempted to capture her, they touched
nothing but a curious dust, which had settled in her hollows.

EAST

Early in February, the wind comes straight from Siberia –
bearing on its giant spine a fine snow.

Easterly is broader than northerly: it may clasp you to death.
Easterly is a bear: northerly is known for its
lupine tooth.

In Latvia and Lithuania, the people rise up with the wind:
thirty degrees of frost do not deter them.
Outer cold and inner heat meet within the
pains of a slow burning; an uncertain birth.

In the Middle East: war.
On English television, speculation camouflages
every insecurity.

The sun, the moon, take turns in a vaporous rising.
Snow and frost remain, wintering the earth.

EISTEDDFOD

Her lessons were twice weekly in a room with an upright,
with a dark green carpet, lampshade, three-piece suite;
with Celtic watercolours. Wearing her threadbare tweed,
her horn-rimmed glasses, she taught with a virginal
voice-and-hand – her perennial test the eisteddfod.

In the West of England Academy's guarded gallery,
we performed on a Steinway; alphabetically. I lacked fluency:
strength came quietly, after the adjudicator – from the father
of prizewinning girls, whispering behind me,
willing continuity; from my consolation tea at the Berkeley.

Of course there were tinier eisteddfods – in mustier halls,
and with high marks as common as evening neon: once
I won a silvered cup, was keenly applauded.
Yet already, I knew that what counted – created
a kind of tacit harmony – was celebrating excellence.

ELFRIDA'S TALE

In the days when pollution remained in town,
when the suburb had barely begun to fatten,
she came to a limestone, countryside cottage.

London-born, nectarine-cheeked,
she lived in the exuberance of her sons;
in the stillness of her husband.

Hardly a jot of uncertainty – envy – could be
spotted in her lane, or on the neighbouring farm.
Each year – home smelt of beeswax, sunned
cotton; the butterfly starred in the play of the hedgerow.

But once town had chosen to cleanse itself, to approach
more subtly – once the farmer believed in
expensive, miracle spray – then the likes of Elfrida, and her
kinsfolk, were spirited away.

EMPATHY

The whole of his tenderness was concentrated: his fingertips
played on her incisors with delicate metal and cotton;
his tempo was andantino.

Pain became as tiny as a pin:
there was a strange kind of dignity in being supine;
in allowing her palate to be lit by a disc of topaz.

Under the influence of another, those most familiar things –
the faint scratching on a chart by a blond-coated nurse,
the whispering below fanlights from an amethyst mobile,

the distinct vibrating of sun on a moon-tinted wall –
might too often, she felt, be the instruments not of her healing,
but of a further hurt.

EPITAPH FOR BOBBITY

The rabbit died warm, without fuss.
He lay for a day on the straw by the bran bowl,
blind and incredibly old.

The child watched brightly,
smiled at the breath that was just, just there.
Death was neither lovely nor ghastly to find,
just warm, without fuss.

EVEN NOW

Even now – in my forty-ninth year –
I am still without appropriate fear
of the lion rampant.

I do not admire him either –
but am resigned, like my ancestors were:
like a marked Holocaust Jew.

Again and again, the lion has mauled my soul:
again and again, I seek a position where I may
take in the slow, dark balm of the mothering sea.

Inland, I find the baby who is innocent and wise;
yet wherever I stand, I cannot see who holds her;
and who becomes the giver – and who the receiver.

Even now – full forty-nine years after the Holocaust –
I do not require a fatherland….
Where is the mother…? Where is the sea?

FEBRILE

I watch the world through Perspex eyes,
from fever-stilts.

Child, how you run! You are bursting my bubbles.
Your rag doll falls.... I have fallen beside it.

Somewhere about us there rises a kindness,
a promise of sealing.

GENTILITY

For half of this Devon town,
Thursday afternoon had an air of convalescence.

The high street sloped generously:
you parked your scarlet car by the recommended front.

The experts – the antiquarian,
and the woman from the lace emporium opposite –
had gone to an auction.

An ex-model advised – her voice more refined than her wares....
She would promise me nothing:
my Victorian sampler was common – could waste for years.

In a tearoom with lamps made of Philippine shell,
you mentioned your extended family, your ideal castle;

while the lady upstairs played mirrors with her hair –
her servant looking no less prepared than the water, the scones.

"GLADLEIGH"

A back-lane cottage – tinted like a Neapolitan ice.
They lived in the strawberry portion.

As soon as you felt the doorbell,
a Welsh corgi emerged from somewhere steep –
all hysterical saliva.

Inadvertently, they advertised their deafness –
their afternoon television fussier than the dog,
the casement fully opened, even in winter;
his hearing aid conspicuous on hairlessness.

Gladys, casting off gentility like stitches,
was usually absorbed by the boxing, the rugger,
her hands continually knitting, not applauding;
while Leighton, her husband, accompanied himself to the garden,
or imagined prosaic posters.

The moment the inherited clock struck four,
tea would be arranged; sun would illuminate
dust on the mirror, a fireplace without flames,
an unwatered cactus....
They were no more disturbed by encapsulating change
than by distant traffic.

GOING HOME

It was then that I returned.
For too long, I had breathed adopted air –
how very rare, how very foreign it had seemed! –
and my mind was unperfumed, and I was conscious of mortality.

It was then that I trod through the lost, the forgotten,
and found an indestructible kaleidoscope
of known faces, known crevices.
All I had dismissed had imperturbably remained.

GRAIN

Emerging from the dimmed rooms of Hardwick Hall –
from those tapestried walls, those numerous, curtained windows –
I am caught by that ripeness of August sun.

Shocked open, I look across the ha-ha: look at the
vivid, stilled hologram of a multidimensional world:
at wheels of cut wheat; at Derbyshire sheep
gracing a distant, dark slope.
To cross over the boundary would surely, suddenly
diminish things....

Three weeks later – emerging from the interior of
Otterton Mill, in East Devon – I am drawn to the
bounds of a second grain field: I enter the gateway,
sense the vitality of maize – high, unharvested;
am balanced between late August sun crests
and light, spiralling river breaths.

Remaining close to the grain,
I am opened no less here, in Devon, than there, in Derbyshire:
opened to ripeness of the Earth – whether distant or near.

GREEN FRIDAY

It is the day of Venus. Green Friday.
During the afternoon, I am taken out to a gymnasium:
here, I am the guest of my son – and of his foster mother.

Inside the building, those humorous fringes and fingertips
coax: they request spontaneity: everyone who comes
jumps, climbs, the lime-coloured net....
At the very first attempt, I clear my fright.

Afterwards – home is a humming-room; lullaby-couch.
But long before dreams, rest is upbraided by those same
mischievous faces and hands – seeking the greenest of
beads: which are found behind my pillow – destined for
reassembly; Saturday's chains.

Southwest of the house, the ocean becomes turquoise....
Venus continues to foster the earth, with those membranes of
viridescent light – in which touches of pain can
hardly be seen.

GUILT

She whispers her untruth to the last twilight tree....
Bent like a patient patron, it listens – and disbelieves.

She bathes her swelling insomnia in the blossom-filled pool –
whose fragrance will not stay.

Inaudibly, behind a limestone wall, she weeps; and weeps....
An owl watches her crouch; turns informative....
"Trespasser, trespasser!" mutter the grasses.

In the morning, she drags her cracked cowardice into town,
and exchanges it for unpatterned bravery –
and rehearses her confession in the granular alleyway.

HALFWAY

The mother, the stepfather and half-stilled boy have
travelled to Bakewell – fifty miles; via Cromford and Matlock.
The boy's father, his wife and their son, have journeyed
just as far – via Hayfield and Buxton.

In the Pudding Shop's upper room,
the mother seeks a resemblance between the father and her child:
scanning their faces, hands, gestures – all she can find is a
slight reediness of tone.

Afterwards, near Tissington Trail – where trains once passed –
the boy with two fathers and two mothers
remains in the car: obsessed, at sixteen, with his
vision of controlling it.

The women walk slowly, well behind the men.
One attends to the other – whose talk is of dogs:
her Yorkshire terrier is let off its lead for the
first time ever.

At Ashford-in-the-Water, tearoom comments
are dropped like intermittent rain. The older boy
feels alone, even facing his half-brother:
alone against adults who speak about dogs – and poetry.

Together, they amble towards the bridge by the
medieval Sheepwash – where photographs are taken.
The waters of the Wye are exultantly clear: there is an
oriental feel to its foliage and wildfowl.

Later, someone will remember the well dressings of Ashford:
how, nine years ago, the Sheepwash theme was the
Chinese Year of the Dog; its design –
the universal willow pattern.

But now – in the five o'clock spring light – they
return to the car park; half to go north; half to go south.

HARRIET AND POLLY

As Harriet Edmunds is wheeled across the salted road,
I watch her blind, intelligent wrists;
and her eyelids – closing to the northeast wind;
and her skein of tawny hair – falling onto her soft, plain cloak.
She leans forward a little, as if in pain or meditation.

Mr and Mrs Edmunds admire: they long to comprehend
the uninherited awareness, the musical compositions,
the ability to concentrate when the ear has grown deaf.
Constantly, Harriet recollects the sighted, heard years –
years when imaginative trust stayed cloudless.

Newspapers, television studios, are beginning to question....
It was not so for Polly Jones. I can still picture her
kneeling in church, clasping a Braille Bible;
waiting for her hand to be touched by a found child:
at least she was not weak-limbed, or hard of hearing.

Orphaned, though thought to be mostly ordinary,
she fixed those listening eyes on no one – even there....
Her plumpness was partly concealed by the dark of her garments:
stone-blind from birth, she had not been permitted
to experience the feel of colour.

HER BELOVED

He watches her from the sepia on the sideboard, the wall –
watches through the eyes of his posthumous daughter;
and through the grandson, who inherits that passion for danger.

For forty years, he has forbidden the wind to blow upon her:
in the evening, he brings her a honeymoon rose on a salver,
and illumines each nook of her house, each clock without a key.

He sees that the awakening romantic novel she is writing
will sell; that all her Teddy bears are adequately patched;
and that his fragrance will be noticed by selected callers.

THE HOUSE ON THE GREEN

Here is a house Victoria has known.
We approach it from the garage: a pentad of friends

climbing past minute pairs of boots
into a plaza of a kitchen –
where Judith, the mother, makes angular pizzas.

Her dining room is clever enough to face south:
we glance at Penelope's artwork, slanting upwards.

Victoria's works go dark in their boxes:
the whole brown in her hair, in her eyes, welcomes
from a seven-year-old photograph.

All at once, Grandfather arrives –
his pink, his blue, matching the fair blue of
Penelope.

Laughter illuminates:
Judith becomes daughter; designer.

It is hours before games go to cupboards –
before the hand touches a warm door;
a firm curtain.

IDYLLWILD, CALIFORNIA

In the moment between dreaming and waking,
the sky needs to be hidden,
the unbidden words furled:
in Idyllwild, a time *long after* the dream
is the time to begin.

Blue jay, robin and woodpecker
witness the dawn –
at one with the butterscotch tang of the pine-bark,
the chocolate bark of the manzanita.

By forest boulders on Mount San Jacinto,
raccoons, lizards, are keenly aware
of wolf, coyote,
mountain lion, black bear.

Now, words fly wild as disturbed feathers;
then swoop like an eagle
thru pure, bare sky.

ILLUMINATION

In my vestibule of solitude, I meditate on light:
I remove every vestige of dread, of self-pity;
I move away the films of sloth, the cataracts of guilt.

As the dawn washes in, with its quantum of mercy,
safely to their graves go the faces of the night –
re-embalmed, and made benign.

IN CONCERT

In the mid-August, modest studio, a family wearing
blue and white stripes plays flute, cello, viola and guitar:
plays Telemann and Haydn; and an Irish tune – *Spancil Hill.*

The music has opened fully as a fan,
quills of it travelling towards visions on the wall –
– towards paintings by the father:

paintings which hold kernels of power – the faintest
signature, gesture, suggesting blossoms of response.

Patient by the exit are tables of Devonian wine:
in the garden below them, stone, wooden, and iron
sculpture becomes both rakish and intense.

Winking through the highest window, is the foliage of light:
it is winking at the heart of this place – where photographed
artwork, influenced by Seurat, basks in narrow albums.

Punctuating the whole experience of artists and guests are
poems by Mother: vernacular; and global.

INEVITABILITY

In the October mauve light,
Sunday families hang about for hours;
despondent;
despite the mature quiet.

After the yellow summer, the iced food,
they tried to be defiant for a moment –
to dance changelessness.

Once they have returned to their aching, high-ceilinged houses,
doubtless they will see how the
winking sun-in-the-mist slowly,
slowly falls, between small, dependable hills.

INFLUENCES

On the second Sunday in November, we found ourselves
winding between south Devon hedgerows –
to what had previously been the engine house.

Years had passed since the mine had ceased:
a wing had been added to the body of the stone
so meticulously that it seemed to have grown there.

Behind the house, the lithe river was unimpeded by
dimplings of rain; elderly sheep remained on
steep pasture; an old chimney accumulated lichen.

In the kitchen, we were nine:
four men, four women, and a baby.
The baby grounded her angel being, slapping the

deep red floor tiles with exuberant palms....
Pain had been shading us all since our last meeting;
but the love still radiated – refined in slanting light.

After a meal flavoured with local herbs and fruits,
some were absorbed by the water, the woods:
others looked into the open fire, felt the presence of

the owner's late husband – one of many
influences in this flowing place: where then was
patiently unfolding into now; and was blessed; and healed.

INHIBITION

His birth element was water: yet only within the
receding dream, the narcotic bathroom, would he
permit himself to be embraced by it.

As though to atone – he would frequently imagine he was
flying above it, running alongside it; and he would plan to be
observer of the ocean – more than of ponds and canals.

At moments of potent imbalance – an element of
death was what he admired; and approached.... Yet
even then – it was a water he could never entirely enter.

INTERLUDE

Between terms, were those long holidays in Celia's
home – on the edge of Somerset: where the quarry seemed even
dustier than television's Wild West;
where the outhouse contained secrets, in paints and varnishes;

where smells were peculiar but harmless. Little was forbidden –
only that disused urinal; and Ivor, with his volcanic
smile: a distant pungency of lunch
waved to us continually.

At the age of eleven, we were far beyond playing at mothers and
fathers: evenings, we lay on identical beds,
listening to the giggling of grown-ups behind
hardboard partitions.

Soon, we should be learning separately – Celia in her navy,
I in my crimson. Celia's mother was noisy about our
scholarships: though her husband remained deceptively
nasal-toned; and heavy-eyed.

INTRUDERS

Conscious of negative ions near the weir,
yet neglecting oblique nettles,
he positions his oblong of plaid where the sun
can hypnotically tan.

Clothed in a synthetic clash of greens,
he closes his lids. I half settle beside him,
observing through Polaroid lenses the reproaching weather –
– in particular, noting that yellowness of mist by the distant

malodorous tractor.... My child yens for triangular
caramel: for his ration of attention.
The cuckoo sounds clouded. We cannot give names
to the riverside flowers, the trees, our feelings.

Intruders that we are, we can nourish no more subtlety here
than those girls among the rushes can – further along;
who compulsively aim stones at a floating bar –
and discover nothing.

THE JESTER AND THE DUNCE

The son, at fourteen, sports twin caps –
one for the jester and one for the dunce.
The former reveals colours of holly and ivy, with a
gold and silver bell: the dunce's cone is a
dense cardboard – February blue; donkey gray.

Mother, who is brittle, who has little time for humour,
fails to bear these extremes of lightness and weight:
continually, she steals the hats – or conceals them.
Till her son becomes tall, a glowering tower,
his upper lip simian: till the atmosphere between them is
charged with word-swords. Till a whole world congeals.

When she would expel him – she dreams of conical hills
topped with conifers and flowers: which turn to an expanse of
steely water – with banks of gargantuan chimneys.
She wakes – only to be confronted by the jester and the dunce
inside her: to be freed, she needs to be loving them.

For what is a dunce but a child of the wise one…?
What is a jester, but a leavener of sorrows?

JUNE

Now she is well past fifty, hay fever avoids her –
enabling her to nurture those foxgloves; to celebrate:
throughout two summers, she will ask for frangible pink
to involve the bees;
will respond to the novelty of pollen-coloured sun.

Suddenly full of how garden and gardener enjoy each other,
her poet friend – whose mind rather than hand
tries to ennoble –
perceives how the life can evolve solely where there is
friction between white and dark; tart and dulcet.

LETTING GO

Travelling north and east
from coast to centre,
I notice the Magritte picture
in a wing mirror:
my head against fine cirrus.

At the fringes of each county –
Cornwall, Devon, Avon –
I hear myself calling out
"Goodbye ... goodbye ..."

I remember that midnight clarity,
for taking leave of
birthdays; Christmas Days.

An ancestor – a refugee –
whispers in my hair.

LIDO DI JESOLO

In single file, we take a self-prescribed path:
one that skirts the kiosk, that raises the heel above raked sand,
and keeps behind the parasols and striped chairs of sunbathers –

who are totally, habitually at ease on their hotel allotments;
unperturbed by excursionary murmurs….
Unfailingly at hand, sun salve is a talisman.

Not maintaining eye contact, quite silent,
we make for the lighthouse – pausing at self-conscious intervals
to gaze at cirrus clouds; or creep along a breakwater.

Many of them sleep, barely aware of the noonday elements:
of how, this June, the Italian sun seems cooler;
or how the sea is like a turquoise frieze – yet never too distant.

They do not observe us turning the corner; or discover how
exhausted we are by the harbour: we wait behind closed lids
for that spinning disc of lights – which, later, we shall discuss.

In front of their flat-roofed, immaculate hotels, they are still
totally at ease. A disc of lights is recorded within them too –
somewhere…. They are beyond striving; or analysing.

LIFE REVIEW

A mother attempts to videophone her son:
because of one half-broken button,
nothing is to be seen.
However – fancying she hears the
whispering of companions – she tries again.

All of a sudden – visions begin:
in the first – the schoolboy of nine crouches in front of a
stage hearth: others in the class, it seems, are chosen for
drama-without-scars.
Mother, like son, is the unobserved observer.

In her vision of the six-year-old boy by the sea –
toying with a watch that she has given him – she catches herself
stealing it back; and passing it on….
Recalling that northeast wind at the end of August,
she learns about his sense of unreality.

In a third vision – he turns into the baby in the grass:
becomes the imago; the six-pointed star….
When he jumps his wordless patterns into unlimited air,
she feels how he concentrates the wisdom
here and there; here and there.

At last, the videophone reveals him, fully nineteen –
– rejection pressed into withdrawn pupils:
beyond them – are signs of a dying star….
Finding its pulse – the mother begins to listen:
to respond in time.

THE LIGHT AND THE DARK

Not a mile from tired sea, and under a waning moon,
she creeps down a steep hill; is still heavy with day.

Continuous traffic disturbs her step.
She reaches the chosen college, promised room;
walks to her allotted table, the novel in her hand.

The tutor, who is the gentlest of scholars,
illuminates countless domains of the mind....
Colours become subtly relevant:
William's gold hair, Veronica's red scarf,
Catherine's enthusiastic cheeks.

This novelist, this genius whom they discuss,
would harness the whole of hell; whole of heaven....
For a moment, they seem to be harnessing with him.

LOOKING IN

The box comes alive: her favourites are the pink and mauve
cardigan buttons – the diamond ones, with lily of the
valley in their crevices. She collects light in these.

Till something inside her protests, jealous; jounces
up and down, up and down: till the taste on her
palate is of staleness – like that of toy metal.

So after her lukewarm milk – and her biscuit, peppered with
holes like a colander's – she is glad of a blanket and cottons
to darken the evening.... Once underneath them, she imagines
saffron stars, expanding and contracting; then a doorway on a

mountain. Then continually, feeling even higher than the pine –
she listens to an atmosphere rehearsing its aria; finds
countless variations on her friends and acquaintances,
pulling uphill to accompany her....

However – she cannot, cannot enter it fully, this dream;
she can only look in: her foetal position is laughed at.
Very soon, she encounters a blinder, kinder sleep....

Early in the morning, she is glancing at those buttons again;
collecting a perfume of lights: dancing the pinks and
mauves; greens and saffrons.

LOW TIDE

It was the mist we noticed first –
gothic on the cliffs.

Later, when we promenaded,
everything seemed to be slipping away:
the autumn tide had receded,
had left a faded sand to expose ungarmented last hopes;
the afternoon town was a husk,
half filled – with enervated sun, with diminished wind;
and even when the unwinding-within-walking was over –
even then, we found our surroundings disturbingly unchallenging.

We remembered an intense artist who had lived here once –
remembered aloud:
we imagined that by doing this,
we could add a little substance to the place.

MACHO

An Argentinian Jew –
who believed in the inferiority of women –
he remembered how his first wife had faithfully accompanied him,
truck-bound, for a thousand crooked hours;
and how his widowed mother, though frequently making do,
had obediently offered him sweets of
sweet potato, dark chocolate and halva.

A postgraduate scientist,
usually he was drawn to the tonic plains of the intellect:
friendship failed to intrigue; colleagues were interrogated.
Only a few of them glimpsed that intermittent, nervous tic;
or surprised him setting opaque poems to music.

With metal in his eye – and in the ivory and ebony of skin and hair –
he moved from continent to continent, constantly
honing himself: his element was fire.

He could never, never acknowledge any fear.

MALAISE

The Sunday after Easter – my almond-green living room.
Your throat hurts; your eyes feel
hostile towards daring light:

when I have drawn the fawn curtain, you can taste
buns without crosses; scones.

The curtain is too high; it reminds me of a
huge-pupilled iris, turned upwards – of that
white, maddened beneath.

I am no less disturbed than at my hairdresser's – where,
recently, an assistant placed semi-opaque
plastic on a client:

to tease out, through minuscule holes, her most
serpentine filaments....

You come to my west room: light sympathises:
your dark, against my bald window,
turns to ash blonde.

MARIANNE

We are lost – or found – in this meditation centre: are the oval
around the crystal – around purple for Advent,
or Lent.

The frailest in the ellipse is Marianne, the potter – who endures
tumours on her liver: whose eyes have become much more
luminous than any quartz. She is dressed in contemplative
blues.

I imagine the unchosen cells – orbited by a blue and white
fizzy light. To the owner, death seems as youthful as her
grandchild: it is the crony in the valley….
Distance is irrelevant: signs and destinations are at once
very far – and very near.

From outer space, Great-Grandmother Earth can only be
partially seen. She remains, in her bubble of blue and white,
mostly benign – despite the violation, the neglect, which make her
contract inwardly;
or expand in the wrong places.

MASQUERADE

Light of head and light of toe,
up and down, up and down the wine red stairs they go;
while far below, on sullen stones, he listens.

Pine burns in the iron grate;
they busy their tongues with irrelevant flavours;
their bloodless hands fuss.

He walks outside, where fellings and killings have occurred;
where darkness becomes less dumb;
where the air of the Old Year pierces him.

He watches them leave, noisily exhausted.
A woman turns to stare –
then smiles, as though at a camera.

When at last he is reluctantly admitted
to the cold sweaty tobacco and meat,
he catches a glimpse of acquaintances – closing things;
locking up unholiness.

MEMOIR

Just when her father was drowning in the Avon,
Fiona MacPherson was cycling downhill.
I know because I saw her, still in her school gabardine,
her blondness dressed in a crimson hood.
It was Friday afternoon: dog-walking time.

The morning papers were saturated with it:
the unmended railing, the learner driver, the plunge into the river.
Mother left her cereal bowl at once – to weep in the hall;
and all I could do, meanwhile, was fail to be less jealous
of a popular fourteen-year-old; an emulated beauty.

On Sunday, conditioned not to be too curious,
everyone else was discussing the news in whispers:
not only MacPherson's accident – his discomfiting, first drama –
but also the change in his daughter; those elements of silence
which made her seem remote.... I resembled her less than ever.

MINIATURES

Earlier today, they woke me to glimpse them at my door –
miniature folk –
a boy with a blue and white shirt, and a whistling companion.

Focusing with lids half closed, I tried to
cry out – but the power had already failed.

I remembered Mimi – that blonde doll of a child
who had played hide and seek behind my mother's headboard;
recalled how she had disappeared when the world said,

"Goblins and ghosts exist only in dreams."
As if dreams were of no importance.

Portions of me disbelieved: quite often now – in a compact
moment between one awakening and another – I quicken to the
honed tune that tells me they have come again, those folk.

I needed – earlier today – to feed them no less than the
whole of my energy; whole of it – what little I had.

THE MISFIT

Saturday afternoon. Nineteen fifty-three.
The petroleum company's annual party.

Annabel, a mechanic's foster child,
totally repelled by the yellowing dishes
of tinned pears and vermilion jelly,
stares: through narrow windows.

No jocular balloon, no compulsory singsong for *her*.
Please…!

Aching to escape from inappropriate gifts –
the outsize box of inferior colours,
the ritual doll with vulnerable hair –
she makes for the corridor.

Here, on hessian, she sits in restorative half-light;
and imagines she is listening to an engine – which is indigo –
pulling her away; pulling her away.

MOAT HOUSE, OLVESTON

Near Thornbury Castle and Aust Ferry, there was first
Tockington, and then, Olveston.... I approach the
long-forgotten familiarity of Church Lane:
its turns and gradients.

Over thirty years on, Moat House looks heavier,
rather than lighter. Its occupant answers the door:
Reginald Crouch; recently retired Methodist lay preacher;
ninety-three.

He does not know me, but recollects my late parents;
together, we remember his late wife, Daisy;
through her, I remember myself – my inner child:
I bring my stilted past into the doorway of the present.

Daisy, fresh as infancy, is imploring me to play more,
to put on shorter dresses; to be open-throated.
Moat House has an aroma of home cooked meals,
floral soaps, pre-motorway hedgerows.

The place seems heavier now, like its owner: who slowly
uncovers his past; embraces his present – those visits from
middle-aged sons; grandchildren. Safe on his threshold,
safe within the frame of Methodism – he begins his goodbye.

MORIBUNDA

Beyond the half-lowered blind,
is the hypnotising tripping of the rain, upon stone;
is the paining ascending of continental aeroplanes.

Very ill, she feels how a small portion of herself strengthens;
and is aware of the displacement of the always-decaying.

And yet, in this oblong, spare room, timelessness is constant.

Forgotten is the extrovert vibration of her past:
all about her is blue; green; still gold.

Cleansed cypresses lean against fences.
She rises; and raises fully that hard, pallid blind;
and hastens through many a window; many an atmosphere.

MOSTLY ALONE

Mostly alone, in the midst of stained commuters,
she finds in every corner of those darkening compartments
his intercity, ocean-searching eyes.

Much of his radiancy lingers in her face:
strangers, at whom she compulsively smiles,
smile at each other immediately – seemingly astonished.

Indigo high tide. Turning away from the train, the town,
she notices neither the wind nor the cold:
the movement of her mind is unusually smooth.

Reaching her porch, she pauses: to listen again
to the known consolation of distant valley engines;
to imagine benign mountains; to imagine she can lift like a leaf-wave.

They confront her – the Madonna blue door, the monastic flat.
Reluctantly, she inserts her tiniest key....
An exact year ago, he was alive.

It is more than half a decade since she saw him....
She gives herself permission to be lenient tonight;
and concentrates on subtle flavours – cinnamon, camomile.

MOTHER, DAUGHTER

Tuesday the seventh of August: in the dampened grounds of the cathedral
I have kept my appointment and found my Jewish mother;
and my youngest aunt; and their violet-eyed companion.

It is thirty-eight years since we parted – Sylvia and I;
yet now I feel no sudden gift, no withdrawal of energy:
the first conversations are strangely easy.

The three of them, all in their sixties,
look quickly for a darkened inn where they can smoke.
They talk safely for a while – about furniture, jewellery.

But once in the pub, Sylvia, with curious intensity,
begins to compare jaw lines; and hands; and feet:
afternoon novelty alone cannot satisfy, she learns.

I, who have seemed to be mostly air and water,
become partially earthed – and less mysterious:
I try to remember the names of my ancestors –

Abraham, Reuben, Harry, Frances;
the geographical details – Minsk, Russia.
And I think of my Jewish father – our hazel eyes.

Before Sylvia leaves for Illinois, I shall give her my poems:
in exchange, she will offer her choicest American perfumes....
Caring, wary, she must prepare herself for more than one journey.

MOVING AWAY

Shortly before the journey, there comes the final salutation.
His compulsive, ultimate walk is like a handshake:
it settles matters.

Yet how pleadingly the town suddenly shines!
How wholesomely astringent the heat becomes!
And how the emptied home hums! –
like some creature which is caught between inertia and exertion.

His neighbourhood is all courtesies.
Enmity evaporates;
and friendship makes impressive, naïve promises.

Moving away, he senses his roots' last lifting; and is ecstatic....
It is a moment of dismantlement, and rest, and reassembly.

NEAR AND FAR

At the close of May, poets converge in a
pub like a buffet car: launch richness of tongues
for Africa – poorest in water.

Between readings, a band sluices conversation.
He who is the main poet joins in the dance:
she, polluted by the noise, buttons her raincoat.

At night, unsealing her soul in the cold hotel,
she dreams she is walking beside him through a deep,
dry gorge.

In the morning, he breakfasts fully in a thin-roofed back room –
talking of sensuality: she responds with metaphysics....
Neither is visibly moved.

As the one bus bears them on its route to the station,
she observes him assisting encumbered mothers –
observes that he is plump-hearted, subtle-bearded.

On the railway platform, he kisses her cheek: before long,
their twin trains will have crossed the river – destined for the
far southwest, far northeast.

NEPTUNE'S DAUGHTERS

Dream-walking on to the campus of my heart,
I am lost.
The heart cannot be honed like thought:
lessons to be learned are without timetables, indices.

Outside the iced wall that Neptune saltily eats,
the small town sells many maps, many clocks;
and I find my level way to the boundary
between town's end and sea's tumultuous start.

An ageless longboat – without sails, without oars –
is tossed to untimely dying by twilight's violets and grays....
A second boat, alive with oarswomen,
glides into sudden sight by harbour walls....

My sister from over the water –
you have opened doors in a number of walls:
now, look into my campus-heart;
into my hushed brightness.

NINETEEN FORTY-NINE

In the post-war parlour,
the old women sit knitting with arthritic, thrifty fingers,
their idle imaginings half grasped by the one child.

She plays on the austere linoleum by the bay window –
almost mesmerised, by over-distinct voices,
by the delicate cups in the heavy mahogany cabinet.

Why do they talk of their daily deeds with such geniality –
these who have known bombs and bereavement?
Surely – there is a conspiracy.

Suddenly – their bravery, their fear, are no longer concealing….
The child picks deliberately forgotten pains as though they were daisies –
and makes chain after chain.

NOVEMBER 2ND

All Souls' Day: day of my birth.
Alone, I come to the asylum-hotel.
Belonging to all time here, I stand in the foyer,
and glimpse from the edge of my vision
the admission of a young man –
his chaos controlled by tranquillising giants,
and behind dark glasses.

Climbing a number of flights of
hastily narrowing, spiralling stairs,
I arrive at where a white-clothed proprietress
pauses – matronly in her smile:
in her denial of dislocation – of the door
locked and bolted; the opaque window.
A nurse lingers – out of her view.

Descending the back stairs,
I find myself in a tunnel, barely lit –
its walls and ceiling unplastered, revealing
the unique fragrance of psychosis....
Along this forbidden corridor, shrivelled creatures
mutter and shuffle. I cannot communicate:
I observe.

Before my throat tightens – even before I have
spoken your name – you are coming towards me,
sister of my soul: your fairness seems an illumination….
One by one, all subterranean guests are
moved by your stillness: you unlock them; unbolt their doors.
Male and female, they follow us patiently –
climbing that straight, wide staircase

to the nucleus of the house: a landing facing east
where an arched, stained glass window admits
a whole birthday of light through its red, gold and blue –
engendering presents of energy, clarity, communication….
You have asked for the woman in white to join us:
we form an expectant crescent. From clearest sky,
sunlight taps, taps the brightly stained.

NOW

To know with only the left brain – the analyst's tool –
is a foolish business: a knowledge walled in.
To know with the bone, the heart, the intuition,
is a matter beyond dimension.

Emotion, like weather, is an unremitting flux;
time and time again we are drawn, drawn into a vortex:
till we sense no more than the shadow of our future;
the duskiest of dreams.

Words are in memory of the present: become the
afterthoughts of paradox – constantly releasing and
concealing. "Now" is a syllable yelled in the wind:
memorable.

Without the quiet knowledge of the centre –
whose present is not between past and future –
the pain of the vortex is unbearable; unplaceable.
Yet now – we are shown how to suffer; to bear: to be borne.

THE NURSERY

When I was thirteen,
when my mind hurt with Latin unseens and theorems,
when lunchtimes became petty,
I would leave the classroom, hall, kitchen,
would climb past staff room and green room, and enter the nursery –

where the starched matron was unconcerned with analysis,
with academic fashion shows.
I would lie on the ottoman, staring at the white paint
of cleansed cupboards, a glass of kaolin near my hand,
my throat constricted by the nameless phobia in charge.

Convalescents came and went: Fiona, with the magnolia
knee; Rosemary, light pirouetting in her eye.
I learnt to listen to the assistant, Olive Broomfield,
who talked about Ireland, her homeland: about mountains; moss;
tubercular blood.... Softly, I would acquaint her with my poems.

OBERAMMERGAU

Here, in the lemon honey of the mountain air,
and between frescoed chalets, is a geometry of logs –
economically stacked: in each region of the village
there lives at least one family of woodcarvers.

Abrupt against a May blue sky, stands the grayest of
theatres – with an interior like an aircraft hangar.
A fanfare summons today's playgoers – in a tone of
measured rapture: they come obediently from
punctual coaches; they assemble on washed paving stones.

The Passion Play, with its blond-robed, choral formality,
seems fully controlled. Beyond continual movement,
beyond an appropriate music – far out in the open –
curtains are occasionally parted: disclosing the
very core: the concentrated stillness of a tableau.

OCTOGENARIAN

Halloween. Five o'clock leaves fly into her windows –
where decades of steam, storms, have rotted whole frames.

Agnes, tutored by thrombosis, waits beneath a
candlewick pink which fails to match her condition.
On her chest of drawers – the rouge will be unused,
the telephone button remain unpressed.

Relentless as death, she turns down that offering of
screens and speakers: basics alone are required:
the immaculate commode; the bottles of medicine,
murkier than soil; the modicum of food.

Her husband – whose builder's bones are preserved in a
country churchyard – nudges her bound mind:
"Let go! Now!"
And mind examines the hastening winter of flesh.

It remembers her lifetime of labour – as milkmaid;
butcher's assistant; half-acknowledged family nurse:
it remembers the feel of potted plants, Somerset gardens.
This is her first significant illness.

A neighbour embraces her hands – hoping that, even
now, she might cease clotting the flux of love.

ON A WELSH MOUNTAIN

Once upon a time, on a Welsh mountain –
the English would have called it a hill –
a large council estate was grown.
It was frequently inspected, during summer, by the willing wind,
the accompanying rain soon driven, like the twice-daily buses,
down to the valley ...

which was a long line flanked by stone –
the stone of terrace houses: darkened, not cold.
Here, ewes walked on the tarmac with their lambs –
looking, looking towards water; awake before the cuckoo.

Miss Caldicott, the Englishwoman,
the one with no money, no work, no relation but her baby,
had been hauled from a valley of coals – to Mrs Rhys:
a mountain landlady, lately widowed,
who had been wedded to pneumoconiosis for ten years;
who now encountered grief within concrete.

These exiles were too frightened to be friendly with each other:
the estate was neither Welsh nor English –
with its global supermarket, and brown betting shop;
and florist's full of foreign blooms.

ON FIRE

Moments after the lane's light has ceased,
negative thoughts are pitched through her living room glass
in the guise of an outsize, Guy Fawkes rocket:
its premature explosion releases a legion of emotions.

As tangerine hunger trespasses on the inner silence,
anger joins forces with terror; threatens to
consume the marrow.

Yet towards dawn, a distancing begins;
at the same time, a strange euphoria becomes:
attention is given to the law, the brigade, the papers;
camera lenses, luminous hands.

Items that matter – her manuscripts, her piano –
simply wear that powdery mourning garb:
they look positively unscarred.

Those fragments of fear, anger, joy, are
swept up by a revived consciousness that
fire – like water – is both creator and destroyer;
and that home – like belief – is at once a haven and a prison.

OUT OF THE GRAY

In the house by the sea, the poet stands awkwardly –
his silver hair untamed,
his eyes containing untimely moons,
his hands too intense, his manuscripts too ashen.

Yet out of this tremulous gray, comes richness –
a richness which the audience fails to applaud....
Distanced, it responds with premeditated questions.

In a corner, confined, is the afternoon sun.

OUT OF TIME

Quite uninvited – he crept into the hotel foyer
to enquire about her January quarters.

Five years had passed since he had last seen her:
despite premature angina, solitude, the changes within his
habitat – little had evolved.

He expected her at least to remember the choir;
the passacaglia; his poems in the midsummer rowing boat:

was taken aback when she appeared in the doorway –
shabby-cheeked; dressed in unseasonable fabric....

Her reaction to the names of previously shared friends –
to his tumour of temper: to his yarns about a
benign mistake – was one of unconcern.

And when he had turned away – she simply remained within the
impermanent bedroom: listening to the distant singing of
hymns: reflecting how aloofly the grape blue came.

OUTING

All of that house was discreetly closed:
only the grounds remained open to November.
On the moist, Sunday hill, towards sunset,
the west woods fully reddened.

Willingly responding to gradations of tone, of texture,
you halted for a while: to listen to bird song, and wind song;
to finger the unique brittleness of leaf and bark;
to wonder continuously at everything – like a small, small girl.

You persuaded me to stand still by the octagonal memorial:
you pointed to a tree: it leaned across the ridged, sloped land
as if it were pained through constant, solitary toil....

Meanwhile, the boys, half oblivious of the masterpiece, the magic,
and pretending to be frightened by a subterranean ice house,
made for the glossiest banks, the immediate stile;
and questioned very little; and absorbed a great deal.

PANTOMIME

After the downhill caution, through January ice,
the town's one theatre seems luxuriously warm.

At once, the child is absorbed in laughter –
evidently still young enough to delight in stereotypes:
the pantomime dame, tossing new confectionery
and old jokes into the raftered air;
the principal boy – who is almost comelier than his princess;
the amateur magician, the clown, the genie.

Five evenings later, he attempts his own version:
what has prompted him, what he begins to discover
is the continuous dialogue between good and evil;
only this time there is just one character –
one without even the precaution of curtains....
The room where he performs is pallid blue, and hardly heated.

His audience-mother, encouraging, silently remembers.

THE PARK

On going back darkly through the narrowest gate –
through thirty-seven years –
I come once again to the aromatic promises
of mown grasses, secure flowers.

Beyond the finished tennis courts and bowling greens,
beyond the youngest swings
near the crematorium's firry screens,
a summoning stranger passes.

Maturing light reveals too many exits....
I look for my mother, my perambulator,
confining myself to what I believe to be
patient foliage, pacifying stone.

PATERFAMILIAS

After that concert moment – his *previous* wife
provides the buffet: it is Mother who drives the familiar
jalopy – Mother who tunes the children; whose hair becomes
light with care.

He rests opposite her now – in his first wife's
reserve chair, by the apple green Formica: he is listening
to Emily Dickinson.

Neither of the wives is denying his power – the power he
conducts: the first concentrates, birdlike; the second
poises. He enables both of them to become
total participants in silence: in music.

It is Cressida's birthday – a Sunday fest for a quick smiler,
a dedicated cellist; yet here, she sits on the lowliest of
seats, hunching over her homework: he will arrange it for her....

Laurence, at twelve, inherits his acknowledging nod,
his leonine expression. Anthonissa, the youngest, comes straight
to the centre: it is easy for her – this extempore relating;
this playing with another.... Meanwhile –

pelleted words are turning into thistledown; the wives are sipping their jasmine tea. He continues to read – valuing the presence of silence: of music.

PERCEPTION

The older be becomes, the more sun he lets in:
he has learnt – still learns – what to leave out....
At the end of a late winter's hush – paintbrushes wait in a
kitchen jar; in the zones of windows.

For decades director of theatre, opera,
he has only to concentrate once to make sense
of a twelve-year-old, visiting boy: to find
complexity in the fine vein; quickness in the bone.

Recalling his own boyhood –
the lack of communication with another –
he imagines what might coordinate hand and mind
before heart can contact heart: suggests computers.

His wife – enthusiast, earth-toned – places
tuna on the rye bread; buns on the round table.

PERDITA

Although I have entered the ancient heart of a wood –
and have circled it for hours –
I cannot find a source for
this crying of a baby:
a crying without a crescendo; without rest.

Suddenly, a lake's broad face peeps through the firs;
and a white swan floats towards me,
looking me in the eye:
she climbs on to the bank as if to make for the
lakeside well. Thirstily, I follow.

Willing the water to rub from awareness
my nightmare of tears, I find myself
staring through refectory windows: staring past
meals at the hearth; right into the far, far corner –
into the howls of an old baby.

Instantly, as I become her,
I am sucked into the loud light, the pattern of
pains without centres....
Then, half separate, I stand at the refectory door –
and walk towards her; and take her to the
cradle of myself: to the room's hearth:
the cauldron, the ladle.

PITLOCHRY

Walking uphill, they sense the profundity of water:
vitality is heightened; sun lofts are found for
feelings long buried.

At the far end of Loch Faskally, they encounter
strange foliage – strange blooms of
autumn-in-spring. An expansion of energy
starts in the mist – starts in the heart.

Here, arts and sciences combine, in
attending to nature: the architect, the engineer, are
co-creators: the contours of their bridge reflect the
clarity of the water.

Here below – the hydroelectric power station is
continually open. Beside it, the fish ladder,
the parable of the salmon cycle, remind them of
that constant urge to return to the source.

Descending through town, they gently absorb
the stability of dwellings; the craftings of the crofter:
the local stone and wool.

PLAYING WITH AIR

As parasitic stems embroider the oak –
a paraglider pilot begins his attachment.

As a gate brays open –
he manoeuvres the risers,
is a puppeteer with his marionette;
an Aeolian harpist.

Now that he is the bold one,
his canopy cowers and billows
in fits and starts.

Harnessed and helmeted –
so tiny, so new against Cretaceous rock! –
he runs, at last, towards the vagaries
of chalk's precipice:

sprung like a child....

In this moment, he is one with a
hiss of distance between sky and sea –
like a soaring pterodactyl,
like a gravitating angel.

But he finds himself caught between
the currents of abandon and control.

PLAYROOM

Allowing herself to enter fully into her memory,
she found she was standing in a childhood bedroom:
found manifestations of adulthood –
garments, accoutrements –
side by side with decorative shelving of
rhymes, fables.

Gradually, she noticed the doll, the tricycle:
how topaz button eyes began to challenge hers;
how lacquered toes manoeuvred pedals –
till a shift was willed from wine carpet road
to pink linoleum pavement.

One by one, clocks of all ages took time
to divert her attention:
the first remained silent in its slate blue coat;
the second chimed inappropriate hours
that applied to either future or past;
the third, more modern, was plainly precise.

The woman – before she could cry, or smile –
knew she would give her hands to winding, regulating,
arranging, discarding.
This was the playroom of every time, every mood:
as with the hands, so with the mind.

POETS

Poets are interior designers:
they impress their names on our grand veneers;
their words leave holes;
they unpillar our ceilings, unmarble our floors,
unpanel our walls.

Yet suddenly, their strategy is altered:
phrase by delicate phrase, they relent;
their words make whole;
and somewhere within our abysses, they build us
a listening room.

PRESERVATION

"The world outside is closed," the boy announces.
"Look at the door sign!"

His mother observes
the Sheraton, Chippendale, Hepplewhite; the ottomans and oil lamps;
the mahogany table perpetually set for four;
the weighty ornate mirror suggesting
a careful amalgam of motives, a regulated pace:

while her escort-cum-guest buys a chestful of books....
Like his father before him, he values most their durability.

In this dilatory light,
the high street's passing cars are speedily forgotten....
The retired major, who owns the shop,
smiles with acceptance, speaks in tempered tones;
remembers, without effort, a multitude of lives.

PROJECTION

It is nineteen years since she has known a wide screen:
now, surrounded by the black and silver of a theatre-cum-cinema,
she is frightened she might hurl herself from her tiered seat –
into its uncertain pit. In her gut, are the beginnings of
claustrophobia: in the dominant head, she turns
critic, not participant.

Those characters she observes – at first with reservations –
soon become as magnified as the gods and giants of childhood….
Repression and eruption – blood, and baptismal fire – mercilessly
stir her awareness: even the buds of her hands are unfolded.

Despite her resolve, her once unacknowledged emotions are
entirely at home in flame and flood – in the
chilling and the burning which are separate, yet one…!
Despite her resolve, a hot tear cleanses her cheek.

QUARTET

Under the four o'clock, January fir tree,
he does not know me.
His one hand, drugged, clutches the clammy air....
His skin looks leathery today – looks too old for him.

His Alice-in-Wonderland daughter is punctually free,
her classroom hair turned dull, her steps full of serious trust.
His bicycling son will accompany them soon;
unscholarly and golden; resembling the mother.

Mother herself is enclosed in a one-windowed market.
Modern, in her whites and purples, she sells valuables –
the twenty-year strain well hidden behind painless, business eyes;
and her afternoon voice clearer than the dawn.

RAPPORT

Sally McLennan,
alone on the lawn in her clean linen apron,
feels once more the wholesomeness of blossom, of earthenware,
of mown grass and stone….
She has sown and grown so many things!

Her father – somewhat suited to his thrawn, threadbare chair;
to his room that bears no pastel colour; no flower –
refuses to be touched by her nurturing hands.

Her nine-year son,
totally unaware of any screen, any stained air,
teaches him immediately.

There begins an even finer kind of growing.

REFUGE

In the unit for psychotics,
I am constantly shrunk by the eyes:
eyes like those of the punitive child;
the insecure parent.

The nurse allots palliatives; promises:
she walks with me everywhere.
But in the corridor – I fancy she has caught my malaise:
she hesitates in doorways. Till I lose her....

Acquiring a squat car from the outside square,
I drive without licence – towards the inner city:
towards buses – their foreheads too wide, too narrow.
I am frightened of the ones with fanlight eyelids.

Out of intense nowhere – the nurse appears; takes over:
I steel myself to feel safer.
But resident fear prevents both control and release:
and I lose her again....

After my collision with nothingness, I find myself
standing on the threshold of a huge, rectangular room.
The nurse has not returned.
What do I do? Enter – or leave?

Focusing, focusing on the wall in front, I recognise –
amongst a diagonal of paper hangings –
a handmade pocket of childhood:
I go inside …

feel black and white feathers of the kittiwake, the guillemot:
feel west winds of the North Atlantic
mending my mind, expanding past, present and future
into one; and one; and one.

RESERVOIR

When the basketry session is over, she slips behind
her companions and makes for the reservoir. In her green suit
and cream shoes, she inches through hesitant grass,
a neglected fence hole.

Once on the wall: she counts to ten, then lets herself
slide into the hazel of the water – which feels immediately
too shallow to veil her curls. More amazed than maddened,
eventually she emerges clasped by slime.

But here comes the lorry driver – plucking her off the bank:
canny enough to restore her to her unit – to the cohort of experts....
In time, she is fêted by female attendants – escorted to her
sweetened, second water.

How devotedly they bathe her! When they lift her up in a
stiffened gown – they can tell, they can tell she is more than a
doll.... Most other inhabitants are rather too frail,
too sedated, to contemplate dying before living.

RESISTANCE

"Come; come into my mind," you demanded, "and fatten on theories;
for its larders are stocked with both sweet logic, and savoury wit."

But I saw, through the purposely half-opened door:
the accumulation of manacles;
the knife, continuously cutting;
the sun, being banished from an iron-bound window.

"Come; come into my schemes," you tempted.
And I watched as they burst out of you,
as in their lunacy they tried to catch me.

But away from such tyranny, the hard road straightened, and beckoned....
Weighed down by your own will, you could follow me no longer.

RHYTHMS

Somewhere within that prime fear-of-annihilation –
right inside that peculiar smell which accompanies
certain psychoses –
an artist exists.

Yet even though the Caribbean sister, the doctor, suggest
re-polishing – or have led her to
grand bowls of salvias and a tuned piano –
it is another she needs: the one without questions or quests.

Standing just behind her –
and listening to those chimings from her grandmother clock –
he observes how her shammy does a dance on her looking glass ...

till a moment later, when he bends over her dresser;
when he combs, combs her trailings of hair....

And here – for the artist – it is time for the borrowing of rhythms:
time to compose a little; polish again.

ROUNDHOUSE

A fortnight before Easter, Members of Parliament gather here.
In the basement dark, they appear to be nothing but
giant fluorescent rosettes. With each round of
accusations, their intentions narrow and sharpen.

With a knock on the door – a messenger in white
summons them all to the first floor. Reluctantly
curious, they follow her up the broad staircase,
their eyes pierced by window glitz.

On finding the upper room, each guest
is loaned a white shawl: everything is white.
At a round table in the centre, people sit in
silence – as diamonds of light come through the dome.

Afraid of the quality of such quiet, a few
return downstairs: others are drawn to those arched windows;
to the wonder of that panorama.... And slowly, the rest
join the contemplatives. The rosette is contained by the shawl.

For one or two – total transformation: they feel
themselves – feel the whole room –
pulsing, pulsing with dome-colour: its mosaic
shows on their faces; on the marble of table and floor.

SAFE SUNDAY

After the self-imposed tidying of a sideboard drawer,
the dusting between banisters, the scrubbing of her fingernails,
the attempt to imagine she had become church perfect –
after her doubts had crept into crevices, corners –

she would linger among tombstones, smelling clove pinks on the
marble; would read between the inscriptions how grievances,
grief, were safely enclosed.

Peculiar trust grew within the presence of crisp
clover-and-white hats; or washed plaits
glistening at the undertones of pulpit voices.

The blue cloth, vertical paintwork, proved to her that
God was in his sky place. And then there were signs crying:
"Jesus first. Others next. Yourself
last".... Huge JOY signs – almost bright enough to frighten.

On fine afternoons, she accompanied her parents: learned about
the equilibrium of green, the land's contours; anticipated
buttered crusts.

Fastening the day, came the vesper; the plait of dreams.

SEPTUAGESIMA

Two years and three weeks before her seventieth birthday,
my womb, not my mind, registers her death:
it accelerates my carmine – till her cancer is totally
drowned; benign.

It is three o'clock. Devon.
I sense, with half-bewilderment, how my four walls mourn
in their sea blue paper and saintly paint;
in their green and lilac trimmings.

I sense it – till a scrutinising full moon clears the sky;
choosing for a mask the curtain with a perished lining....
Sylvia, my mother, has pointedly returned to her birthplace in
Hampshire. The sun – *her* sun – comes yawning through Aquarius.

SEVENTEEN PLUS

A summer of magpies and foxgloves led us to
a peacock farm near Powys:
a compact yard, abloom with calves and chickens.

The farmer's wife welcomed us with words
homely as her scones: my son looked pointedly at ease.
The next morning, we would make for the Beacons,
search for the waterfalls.

"I'm not into walking," Alex claimed,
when we hastened along the deserted track;
when we entered the woods.

Yet before long, he was showing us the way:
the sap of adventure was rising in his lean frame,
as the track became a labyrinth of horizontal trunks.

The waterfalls eluded us: the time was not right
for such abundant flow. In the lane near the farm,
the sheepdog rounded us up, showed us the way
home: he was used to the stray.

THE SHOCK

Despite the particular promises of last summer,
it seems that all euphoria has left him for ever.

Where once there was trespassing fire, frost becomes:
as the sun takes its leave of what is ashen, deforested,
even his December self-pity
is paralysed.

Yet into his colourless dreams, rides pain:
ragged;
unaccompanied;
prophesying healing.

SHUT OUT

Somewhere, along this gravelly lane from school,
somewhere you have lost your key;
and disbelief chokes:
gasping, you fumble at pockets, sports bags;
you blame and punish the unlucky door.

And a husband vacuums his matting in the courtyard,
a wife clutches her cradle of washing,
a King Charles spaniel sits in a separate heaven,
sweetly refusing to leave.
Your mother? Is she with the hairdresser – dentist – poet?

You cannot recall.
It is an ordinary waste, the waiting for the first time;
yet the afternoon looks huge: you glance at a spot on the wrist
where burst glass previously lodged –
and turn to collecting a stone or two.

SOLSTICE

On the village fringe, a winter freed from mist
hints at Easter: here, there are fifty guests.

The house becomes warm enough to include a
crescendo of drums, cacophony of clowns; alcoves of silence.

Rituals of the shaman, Amerindian, Christian,
are loose-woven into the dance of
holding fast: letting go.

Luxuriance of laughter – tears – vibrates
over the finite surfaces: in the infinite undertow.

The moorland sheep and pony – bones warning of
New Year frost – feast on lenient grass.

SORROW

Sorrow, you are an unplanned baby:
perhaps if I deserted, you would perish.
How often I wish I could end you with hard words,
the toys of the fearful!
But words would rather injure than destroy.
Your wound-weeping centre would fester, not cease.

Sorrow, you are an unplanned baby:
perhaps if I responded, you would flourish….
And yet – I wish you were cherished in silence,
the zone of the gentle;
for silence likes to clarify, not cloy.
Your name would no longer be Sorrow, but Joy.

STORM

He was ashamed: he had found her on the parquet, alarmed –
her spine supported by panelled mahogany;
her rheumaticky palms cupping the dark.

Even through bone, lightning could communicate:
the luncheon of sweetcorn quiche on a blue and white plate –
the vinegar and honey of life itself – were half forgotten.

A daughter of Nonconformists, and a classical scholar,
she sensed an exposed poverty of ego; felt
knuckles of Zeus become potent as the bolt they enclosed.

Pastilles of discoloured wet fell carelessly from her
son's head: "Idiot!" he said….
Yet she did not mind him finding her there.

TOO NEAR THE EDGE

Walking too near the edge,
by a blue-gold cove of sky,
I yearn, yearn, for a path that is known.

I try not to notice the fragile euphoria of my seven-year-old son;
or the cautionary thorn;
or the ominous precipice.

The inexorable tide turns, turns....
And one of us grows tired....
And one of us is frightened of the palpitating brightness.

On arriving home, we attend to our extremities –
ridding ourselves of the dust; the sand; the tenseness.

TOWARDS DAWN

Towards dawn, the queen can be seen with her daughters –
walking between the deciduous trees from palace to
river. She has chosen the very whitest of her robes –
one that is clasped with mother of pearl. The daughters
inherit this need for brightness – their butter-rich crowns upon
darkening heads. They are accompanied by the peacock –
one that is watchful, not vain.

Each right hand carries a lighted candle:
there are candles in the porches of houses they pass. Here,
they can glimpse the morning star, the crescent moon.
And as crisp as this moon, are the callings of a silver bell
with a gold clapper.

The king remains a lunar shell: remains in the
barque which will bear him downstream to his burial home.
His widow, his children, pause on the bank; they wait for
sun to manifest above the hills: when it does, they
blow out their candles. A flame plays on their faces, in the
form of compassion, constancy. It is even within the
expression of the peacock.

As the gold climbs further and further to marry the silver – the spirit of the king, poised over the bone, becomes light enough to depart....
The barque is unfastened.

TRIASSIC COAST

Midsummer Day, two thousand and three:
East Devon light on the chicks of kittiwakes,
on cormorants and shags,
on the rust red Triassic stacks
of Ladram Bay.

A peregrine falcon responds
to the focusing of eyes:
flies niftily from her cliff nest
to circle the boats.

On Budleigh Salterton pebbles,
naturists lie in a breezy sun:
on the moist sand at Orcombe Point –
the coast's west end –
a kitesurfer takes to her heart
the energy of sky, of afternoon tidelines.

She keeps it for only a second:
she frees it, sending it
high above the water.

TRIXIE AND MO

A woman in dun gabardine comes
brusquely down the hill. In her basket on wheels,
the topiary is a black toy poodle.

Instinctively, most passers-by speak
directly to the dog: sometimes, its owner
responds, with nods of her clipped, sea salt head.
Today, she remains locked in – like an
autistic child.

On entering the corner shop, the butcher's, she collects
prime canine cuts –
and petite tins, suited to her stature.

In the open air – crinkly-haired young girls,
dallying with womanhood,
turn up the volume of their being: turn it
till the pensioner sidesteps; vanishes them….
Her immaculate silence is scarcely touched.

TUESDAY THE COAT HANGER

Fever now distorts … now straightens … makes me a child….
Unable to digest the October air,
unable to accept your unnurtured house, your departure,
I stare at my church of a wardrobe – at its brazen rail.

Seven coat hangers face me: days of the week,
the blue one being Tuesday. And although the colour anaesthetises,
I continue to stare – breathing much faster than before:
this Tuesday is acquiring a pair of shoulders,

a gold head; is a prince clothed in a cerulean
cloak with a silk maroon lining.
And his words are like blades – compelling me to rise,
to go to your garden.

For your home has reopened! You appear beneath the apple trees
moving through the healing grass, your arms full of fruit.
Tuesday softens. We wander in this clove-scented heaven
for hours. Till dusk turns monitor.

Not wanting to see you absorbed by the dark,
I lie on the ground and coax myself to sleep….
In the morning you are nowhere … everywhere.
Tuesday remains dustily in the wardrobe, behind cool doors.

UNA

The children she minds do not notice her obesity,
or the weakness of her eyes behind her large tinted glasses:
they respond to her small voice, her jovial freckles,
her always primary colours.

All of a sudden she is sad; the light changes;
the children are withdrawn; their mothers make frightened excuses.
She half discovers herself in a room with too many entrances:
lathering the tiled floor; fingering the raffia.

"Will no one play with me?" she screams,
smashing a dumb jug....
Yet of course not a soul believes in sour loudness:
someone injects, and directs her to a padded cell.

Later, she is offered paper and pastels –
is expected to express abominable things.
But no: she peoples her mind with infant wonderers,
and sketches nothing but protective, doorless walls.

VANESSA

A clue to her condition presented itself long before her first,
and last, visit to my home: the minute, rounded
handwriting – like a voice too diffident to increase its volume.

Her appearance, on that mid-September occasion, misguided:
a brashness in the complexion, the gray within the hair-gold,
attempted to deny an inner sensitivity; the matronly
folding of well-fed arms consoled a sterilised
womb; within the fallow of the eye, anxiety lay.

The hobby of belly dancing, the regular government job,
kept her from thoughts of her mother, who had committed suicide;
of her father, who was soon to do the same.

She laughed with her whole flesh – as though to banish
once and for all that devil who wished, and wished her to
continue the family habit: to take from no one
but herself.

VAPOURS

On this foggiest of days, she remains quilted.
Despite the radiator, the ioniser, the pillows at her head,
her feet – the curtains drawn over her thin wall of window –
she feels toxic; exposed.

Emotion, thought, lie low: instinctively, she
shrinks further – till her aura loses colour;
is an almond of gray.

Till the deepest bowl fills with cloud – and traps
innumerable small poisons.
Involuntarily, she cries out for light.... Now,
even snow, even a wind-sword, would be kinder than
semi-voids....

And at Candlemas, the first shiftings begin –
the refining of gray; the colouring in:
a lemon-silver sun; a cream-silver birch,
at the end of a downward path.

She rises; opens her window a little: feels the
edges of hunger.

VENICE

A three-dimensional Canaletto! A city of
light and water! Midsummer – yet it remains
tepidly moist. Familiarity encourages warmth,
the turquoise lagoon no longer at odds with quarrelsome sky.

The inhabitants, like the tourists, are drawn into lengthy rain:
they enter into the narrowest of alleyways; enter into the
deep brown interiors of churches; into the darkness which is the
precursor of creation; the domed depth.

Secrets of water scent seep through fissures in stone;
storms have torn at the bridge, have cleansed the orifice:
the indelible street stays linked to the heart of St Mark's;
to the power of square enclosure …

where the Doge's Palace, the Correr Museum, are homes for
enlightenment by Titian; and Tintoretto: where the whole
gold and silver of the Basilica is lit by an
emergent, rainy sun.

THE VICARS' CLOSE, WELLS

Between cathedral and choir school, an archway stands –
entrance to a rectangle of stone:
stone dwellings with long, decorative chimneys;
a road of flagstones, school uniform gray.

Late medieval, it still suggests
regions beyond time; beyond form:
suggests the precinct within the void.

I feel compelled to walk its entire length with
even steps: I am moved by the rightness of the symmetry.

The energy of stone is different from that of
greenwood, or ocean: here, I am neither
aflame, nor in dreams: I give and receive
evenly.

How different from the clasping and losing experience in
towns too clock-tied! How different from the
ecstasy and terror of the wilderness!

In the city outside, sleeping water
encircles the palace: quickened, it wakens the
stone of the streets.

VIOLATION

Walking towards the live end of Fore Street, purposely
alone – I arrived at a blue and white terrace house.

Here, percussive sounds hurled themselves from an
emergent first floor.... How prosaic they were –
trailing me as far as a three-doored wall!

These doors were ecclesiastical; small:
their acute heads were no more diminished by
rhythmic volume than by the graffiti at their side.

I climbed further – was gradually claimed by a
portico of buds; by a moistening tissue of moon.

VISITING THE DOCTOR

The child rests gingerly on her chair:
evidently strong enough to be quite unaccompanied,
she is visiting the doctor.

Too old to peer beneath his plaid blanket –
to ask, "Where are your legs?" –
she stares at the hair; at whitening, curling remains.

The doctor's wife – the acting nurse, the humorist –
refers to her husband as "we", even in his presence.
She records every tide of both recovery and loss.

Her patient, till recently without words, and paralysed,
mentions his grandsons; and talks of hardier days:
the mission; his expulsion; the volatile Congo.

When he and the child begin to play noughts and crosses,
the child turns teacher –
her fear of the unseemly, the untouched, almost forgotten.

WARDEN

Yes: we called her Warden, Celia and I,
though her surname – White – was unfailingly apt.

We witnessed the cap and coat, the elderly hair,
the northerly eye that pecked at our inmost secrets,
the pointed voice –

as to and fro, to and fro she marched
in front of the village hall; where the frosty robin
was seen; where the cane came to assembly.
Only a headmaster could have frightened us more.

Once past her, we escaped into the classroom smell
of empty milk bottles and blackboard chalk,
our places punctually known:
for a year, we perched behind crimson ribbons.

At a quarter to four, it was Warden time again.
Then, we would hasten by the parish church,
hasten down the ridged stone of Waters Lane,

Celia permanently roseate – and I …
awkwardly pale, often with blood on my knee.

A WAY OF LIVING

This is the home of Caroline, and Hermione.
Mid-January has come: in its afternoon tints of
sepia and copper, it has come through latticed windows
into a thatched, hillside cottage.

Caroline is an artist; a writer; an actress. A separated
parent, she needs the protection of a oneness that is beyond
expressed belief: she communes with dryads: by a
miniature copse of dark brown flora – a guardian,
mantelpiece angel is playing a delicate trumpet.

Three-year-old Hermione compounds many talents; she times herself
superbly – her eyes rotund against fragile hair:
her laugh, as she tilts towards the sofa, is a magical spiral....
Here – she becomes trustful enough to fall: over and
over; the right way.

WESTER ROSS

Wherever I go, I sense mountains:
pyramids and paps
of sandstone, limestone and gneiss
replenish the psyche.
To watch is to touch.

Lochs live peacefully among them,
purple and turquoise: at Gairloch,
a great skua soars over the boat;
I see a cormorant, a harbour of porpoises;
a gray seal, almost asleep,
her head above the water.

On the horizon, Skye, Harris,
brighten and fade in a thin mist.
In Plockton, the lowest of rainbows
grazes Loch Carron;
the sun turns theatrical,
illuminating a tiny island.

Near the Pass of the Cattle,
Highland cows and Jacob ewes
are unfazed by the passing car –
or by any invader, past or present.

WHEELS

At the turn of the decade – in nineteen sixty –
I was given a second hand bicycle: naming it after the
colour of the paint – Plum – I placed it beneath the hall window.

In khaki anorak and tartan slacks, I kept to the
same route week after week: Stoke Lane,
Reedley Road; crossing the parallel hills to
Stoke Bishop – its fringes and heart.

Here, where my parents never ventured, I explored the
domain of the wealthy: of Victorian Gothic and golden brick –
both harmonising with nature.

I was reminded of preschool, illustrated folk tales:
I remembered Robin – a playmate from those times.
At once, I looked for his present home; finding him – at fourteen –
embarrassed; half broken-voiced.

At the top of Stoke Hill, one ritual was to
feel for that ring of springy grass: to rediscover
belief not only in fairies – Victorian follies and turrets –
but also in the freedom and frame of myself.

WHITBY

Feel, between the illuminated harbour arms,
what powers of life and death have passed – still pass.

Watch – through that whalebone arch below the
captain's memorial statue – how the east cliff displays

charged ruins:
relics of the abbey of St Hilda – the Mother....

Whitby! – with its jet, its whipped silvers and soft golds;
its one hundred and ninety-nine steps:

where cowherd Caedmon, after one vision,
became an estuary of song;

where Lewis Carroll, strolling on rhythmic sand,
rehearsed "The Walrus and the Carpenter";

where Captain Cook unfurled his need for
expansive dreams;

where Bram Stoker, absorbing the same force as
Caedmon, Carroll and Cook, dwelt compellingly on blood;

where fisherfolk, with mended green and orange nets,
continually ply between the Esk and Northumbrian sea.

WILLIAM AND STELLA

While William the librarian hibernates,
while Stella, in Wellingtons, gardens,
I make myself walk between rain-scented lines of deciduous trees –
trying, in vain, to ease the expanding mind into routine's
narrow lanes.

Time and again I reflect upon yesterday's dream –
when every archway, every porch that I approached
became too low….

William the librarian continuously sleeps,
judiciously nourished with words – which seem fluid things….
Stella, wisest among the latest wet blooms,
communes with what neither confines nor excludes.

THE WISDOM TREE

Once in the middle of autumn, Tam and Fern were
learning their pathways: the ways of the forest.
Children of the Knowledge Tree – the forest giant –
they hid their relics of fear within the
hollows of its trunk: became the gymnasts of its boughs.

They noticed – no less than a bound away – how there grew a more
modest tree; thought how foolish it looked by its
muscular neighbour.
Not until wind stung like salt – till dusk
peppered the air – did they recollect home time.

It was six years before they returned: six after the
king of gales. Shocked to smell the defunct wood,
they failed to acknowledge their long-fallen, parent giant.
Only its neighbour – the modest one – stood tall in that
forest's heart: fully matured: revealing strange fruit.

They hastened forward – one halting opposite the other.
As their fingertips met around the tree stem – they felt as though
platinum heat were coursing through them diagonally:
as though sun, dodging round leaves, were seeking their own
solar disks.

No longer in need of a fear hollow – or a play bough –
they remained where they were….
Till Tam became conscious of hunger – hinting at
gathering fruit. However – within her crescendo of dark –
Fern was concerned about routes home.

Nonplussed, Tam looked branchward for an answer:
found daytime fruits had turned into
luminous, multicoloured jewels….
Choosing one lantern for each hand – he began to understand
how, always, there were enough jewels for the journey.

RISE AND FALL

TENSIONS

Love stands before me – both known, and *un*known:
having dream vision, I find in him both clarity, and opacity.

He covers himself in half-rumours –
which I touch tenderly with the tips and lips of things.

His name, like a soft gift, is flown down to the hungry valleys,
only to be part of an insubstantial diet – of gossip juice.

Without a murmur, I release the rest of him,
and am immediately surrounded by unbearably bare beauty:
he has created a perfect, spherical hole within me.

Yet when martyrdom would lodge there, he begins, begins to return –
to teach me how to learn, and lose … and learn, and lose again….
How much simpler indefinite absence would be!
To become, I constantly loosen, and tighten … loosen, and tighten.

PASTORALE

An oboe is heard first – crisp as an apple.
Then a flute – emollient-cold. Like milk.
Then a clarinet – warm and mysterious as blackcurrant wine.

On slopes where restorative air continuously sharpens,
the appeal of the oboe penetrates into the very core –
the refined sorrow unnoticed, except by the keen.

Near the estuary, the resolute flute doctors the febrile summer,
doctors the pasture under the shimmer,
doctors the last life there, the distanced, the softly coughing.

On the edge of the dry gorge, the clarinet calls: "Follow *me*!"

What I seek is a perfect trio: what I find are three fragments –
the ascetic sweets of air;
the determined unsteadiness of water;
the secretive possessiveness of earth.

AN AREA OF FEAR

Down moonless road, up midnight hill,
by slimy stream, and under dank arch,
he who is ahead moves fast; silently....

We travel from district to stone blind district;
we walk beside brickwork which regularly sweats;
we pause – below the breathlessness, the nakedness of summits.
Always, kept between us, is an area of fear.

At last, he enters an anonymous house;
yet just as I reach it, its callous doors close.
Possessively, I listen.
His distinct voice pronounces foreign verbs.

As soon as he emerges, I clutch at his wrist.
How pulseless it feels!
Like a disappointed infant, I loll against an oily wall.
I weep.

Instantly, he stops.
"I am not your god – only your guide," are his words.
And together, we wander to the centre of the town –
where the air begins to lighten.

TORNADO

I undress to the sound of a bone-paining wind,
while the derelict, newly stoned dead crouch around me.

I strip off moderation:
I compete against slats and panels – snapping at emptiness.

I believe I hear the violated town start to applaud me.

It is only the elements – clapping boards together....
It is only the witnessing vulture that matters.

As for the sun, it arrives too soon.
It attends to me like an intense nurse.

Its medicaments hurt.

THE CLOUDS

On the first day of learning –
the ice blue blaze-of-noon is uninhibited.
Visiting panic has yet to inhabit me.

On the second day of learning –
the cirrus looks lost in such an open-plan sky.
My petite pain is born.

On the third day of learning –
the stratus and the nimbus arrive.
They depress.

On the last day of learning –
the polychrome cumulus visibly swells:
and prongs of orange lightning split the larch.

And I fall underneath it….
I am thoroughly, thoroughly marked – not dead.

THE SLOW FIRE

Behind tall glass, I concentrate on a bruise of sky above balding elders.

All I can feel is a tendril of east wind
spiralling down the inward wall;
lingering in the cranny.

Tired, I hide.
I yawn beneath the nonchalance of dyed yarn.

Resignedly, the world outside slips, slips into its oldest gray worsted,
and almost, almost stops.

The slow fire within me is an annual affliction.
The clock, in its befogged, forgotten room, barely ticks.

A discarded yolk, the sun turns toxic.

TOWARDS LIVING STILLNESS

As soon as December begins –
the smooth white rugs are removed from the floor of the sky,
and are replaced by a poor, porous mat.

On the fungoid ground beneath it, above secret roots, I stand motionless.

The cold would snap at me like a hound.
I let its tongue just touch….
It tastes nothing.

To the east, a child protests.
But the wind sleeps on; the sound dies uncarried.
It is the cry of the unborn.

To the west, the sun descends privately.

A torchbearer runs towards me.
"This way!" he urges….
And longing for that conflict through which living stillness comes,
I follow him.

THE TEST

The child arrives too soon – his garland in his hand.
"Come," he commands.
And he tugs me over a slothful hill.

Whose are those bones…?

They are the bones of the abased, the dispersed –
the leavings of a violent, decadent decade.

I discover further horror:
it is not on the murdered that I am made to concentrate, but on the murderer.

"Go on – feel!" says the child.

How my senses disobey!
Within sudden, black silence, I suffer the weightlessness of terror.
I would taste my tears – but cannot.

Entire, interior winter….

The pardoning light, and the first voiced harmonies of spring, then return;
and cleanse; and involve.

RISE AND FALL

Summoned by an unblemished humming, I rise, rise drowsily through abrupt air.

At dawn, I witness the others ascending.
From every cavity of every sphere they come.
Even the unsound are borne outwards....
Till the galaxies are pinion-patterned.

On the crust of each planet –
blackness is broken into;
the word sweetens on the stubborn lip;
and he who once expelled, once exterminated, runs to his window exclaiming,
"Look! Angels!"

At dusk, there is a timely rallentando....

Dreaming all the while, I drop, drop downwards into the renovating night.

A YEAR OF DREAMS

BLACK DOVE

New in the winter, I sleep in your hand –
a tiny blind dove, different from other doves,
black, born black,
not knowing the light from the egg-womb's darkness.

Lift me to your heart for the sharing of rhythms;
burn away the blackness with breath of white tongues;
feather my wings for the first independence,
and keep closed my eyes.

I come to be rested, readied for spring.

SUNFLOWER

Then came a hurricane, sudden, with sword.
Sunflower was kidnapped.
"Behold," laughed Sea,
"though I spread you with salt for the sluicing of wounds,
though my movements come centre to centre with terror,
I lend you my rug."

"Hush!" beseeched Sunflower,
and then came a lull. Sea grew green;
a petal was yawning, revealing a gold both rare and raw.
But Sun caught its eye and the flower became safe,
investing that gold in a winking water.

CANDLEMAS

He enriched the dawn with jewels of prayer
and the temple of Earth with bells.

He coloured the morning with dreams of green
and the noon with murmurs of mauve.

He clothed the evening in indigo clouds
till they met with the black bier of night.

And Simeon listened, candle in hand,
awaited the birthday of light.

SEA LORD

Child was a soft toy, eyes moist as antelopes',
noiseless with trust.
Shark was a wall, impassive, austere.
But where was the Lord of the Sea?

Child was a worry encompassed by coral,
a fossilised frown.
Shark was a girdle of sinister smiles.
But where was the Lord of the Sea?

Child caught a fear, which was waved into plague
by the black wand of death.
Shark was repentant and healed her with tears,
for the Lord of the Sea was within him.

LION AND LAMB

Maim not my mind with your leonine nail,
but unravel the tortuous skein of my thinking
with chastened hand.

Beat down my proud door with truncheons of confidence;
fill up the dyke of my cindered intentions
with freshets of love.

Praise to the lion
who devours not, ignores not the gift of the lamb.

SONG CIRCLE

Make me your bairn, my laird of the looms,
for one is the weaver and one is the web,
but both are the priests of the cycle of song.

Allow me a lull, my lullaby king,
for one is the crooner and one is the slumber,
but both are the priests of the cycle of song.

Prepare me a cairn, my steward of stones,
for one is the craftsman and one is the crown,
but both are the priests of the cycle of song.

DEMON

There is fire in your rock, a demonised Vulcan,
writhing its river of lava and sulphur,
rending your ribs with its raucous requests,
masking with rich heat my fear-stilled field.

Rocks rise phoenix-like; fields lie in sackcloth;
people come quietly from lost little caves.
With softest of soft days the water nymphs bless us,
for Vulcan has cursed us with cauldrons of change.

THE PIT

Conscious of dross, of ravines between miracles,
watching the dust cloud discolour the sun,
knifed by a diamond of frost, I had died.

Death was a tunnel of soot unillumined,
an eye with no pupil,
a fast-dyed remembrance, risen in a nightmare.
Flesh spoiled first, then the bone became chalk;
skeletal fingers picked dirt from the dank walls,
veiled me from vultures.

The pit.

And after the vespers came fastings and feasts,
and a vase for the past,
and an urn for the night,
and a chorus of kinsfolk with laudings of love.

INVOCATION

Engage me a grave with the bones of old crows,
for the Gross Wing is poised to obliterate light.

Bespeak me a coffin, a cage on the moor,
For the Claw grows grotesque in its lust to molest.

O thou who art Dove, deliver us from Raven,
For his is the thornbush but thine is the nest.

DANCE

Dance to the starlessness, caretaker toe,
the sea's bass drumming, the seeds in the slough.

Dance to the redwood, my hoist of a hand,
the bird's first plainsong, the blooms in the blitz.

Dance to the haloes, my Hallowmas soul,
the scherzos round sadness, the zest around death.

PALM SUNDAY

Gold Flower unfolds,
peeps from its frondage, its afternoon pond;
silvered rock quakes with an April expectancy;
thonged feet tread distantly, rhythmic, processional;
freckled birds sing.

Filled with the fragrance of lately mown gardens
and washed with the Easter wind, Flower is refreshed.

Men come from Sunday cells cowled and sequestered,
their palms and hosannas resplendent as psalms.

A POSTWAR EASTER

A postwar Easter, a second wind Christmas
that hails its old heel on the westerly wall.
Dark cars move stiffly in elderly streets;
the whistling of trains becomes softer than chalk;
floors feel unfriendly; windows are moonless:
they mix me a nightmare in cotton cold sheets.

But morning unbuttons my blizzard-bound childhood,
dissolves it in sun.

SILVER TREE

When flesh feels deadened – the seamstress of evening
brings thread for a cloud.

And cloud blinds mind to the night's stone womb,
the day's gold nails,
weeps on my pillow a parent's safe salve.

Sleep grows silver hairs, whitens with moonshock,
finds me a tree for the ripening of dreams.

WHITE WAVE AND MOON ROCK

White Wave arrives with her belly of sun.
She encounters the Moon Rock, noisily nags him;
she scatters his dustcoat of pearls.

But at late low tide she is seen
lying prone as a sea otter's pup.
Dancing her dreams,
she safeguards from grazes the granite's gray head.

Moon brings a sleeping suit. Sun sanctions play.

WIND VERSUS SUN

The hand on the field is a shiver of sunlight:
the brittle-backed land is a spectre of life.

Closed in a nightshell,
it hears the long fingersteps whisper of whiteness,
feels the bunched palms on its eyelids of grass.

Wind is a whiplash, astringent with power –
a crab apple fear in a frostbitten bone.
Sun protests steadily,
wrests from the wizened field seedlings of gold.

WITHOUT ANCHOR

Without anchor, the boat shifts queasily,
squirms in her mud shoes;
she heaves her youthful guts towards the immaculate bowl of sea.

Wantonly the man slips into her timber arms;
he wrestles with water.
This maelstrom of a morning is breathless, collapses.

There is torture by heat in a syringe of sweat;
there is torture by cold in a spoonful of sores;
there is torture by time in decanters of dust.

The tidal clock ticks with impeccable diction;
the boat sits sighing;
the man lifts his feet from the slough-lure of sleep,
stiffly turns homeward.

REQUIEM

Soft as a quilt,
the Lord Dove descends on the shoulders of trees,
brings for the wing's hurts a hawk's head of oil.

Breasts are emblazoned with hunger of huntingbirds,
talons made brazen round plump summer boughs.

Black Dove is dead:
the husk of her childhood is shrunken, unsunned;
the eagle-gold soul is as stilled as a Grail.

EPITHALAMIUM

Serenely she kneels, this wisp of a nymph,
her laughter, like water, encircling his waist,
her eyes green wells,
her mollifying hands on his sun-smocked brow.

Night is a pest:
she blisters all sleep with her last sullen wind,
her envy unleavened.

Rock is untroubled:
he fashions a nest from his vast vest of moss.
Water Nymph drafts him a dowry of kisses,
weaves him a morning gown fastened with vows.

THE SHADOW

It comes uninvited – a shadow unshriven.
The little bland men with respectable voices
recoil from the hairfall, the hostile tread.

Its habitat changes; its victims are chilled;
they run like the summonsed, with remnant-security,
bump against ugliness, helpless as moths.

Beware of the monster that moves in the mind,
the darkness that lurks in the light!

MIDSUMMER

The dialect of Winter is almost forgotten:
Summer's cupped hands become swollen with promises;
rhythms of evenings are swathed in her gloves.

In the long legs of trees,
in the full lips of lakes
there is language of redness.

Midnight arrives with a shortage of darkness;
she makes do with sunblinds from Yesterday's junk.
Tomorrow looks tall;
predictably hungry, we yawn for his newness.

A TIMID CAT

On the wall by the river there passes a cat –
weird, in her footfall, as one who is haunted.
The stone speaks out:
heedless of phantoms, he holds back the tide with his masterly arm.

She arches her fear;
it is shivered;
she crouches.
The gentlest of grasses and mosses attend her.

The river revives her; the wall is her prompt:
she plays on his shoulder like newly wound wool.

METAMORPHOSES

The beach wears a west wind on its dawn-pimpled skin.
As Conch, I am shifted hither and thither from dune to dune.
The wind's loveless kiss, the farce of his embrace
send a chilled and raucous sound around my head.
Brittle, I am too afraid to shiver.

As Sapling, my straight green strength is well rooted.
Lustily the wind snaps his fingers:
I snap back at him with my branches;
my leaf-hair discolours, is wrung dry;
it falls wanly to the ground.
"Bend or decay!" the command.

As Whitest of Wings,
my power is a wonder in a wound of cold air.
Now may I meet the wind force to force,
laugh in his blind eye,
bounce on his back, on his belly,
battle, race, chase, play,
compulsively dance –
as one swims with abandon in vastest of waters.

Exhausted, I turn Tunnel – an underhand sack
for the dusty damp, the gluey rot of the wind's worst garbage.
Here there are littlest of lights....
The Conch of the morning is a virgin – compared to the mould of the night.

As West Wind himself,
my insanity drives through the hours like a virus:
I shatter the shell;
I burst upon boughs;
I wet, then I fever, the bone.
I scowl as I scour;
I hide inside greed.

But when, like a half collapsed lung, I surrender,
and when I am stunned, then made slumberous with pain,
and when I have shrunk to the size of a snail
comes the Conch on swept sand – like a Salvador Dali.

* * * * * * * * *

This second Conch, my child-father,
promises a gentler end, a holier beginning, than before.
I accept its hospitality.
It is alpha and omega, coffin and crib –
– where the dregs of a penitent wind become dreams.

THE CLEANSING

She brought him a thimble of milk from his childhood,
her breath on its bony rim timid as down.

He chose her a chalice that steamed with her youth;
it boasted of bridles round wrathful brown heads.
Gold-soft he watched: he would win her.

She lent him a tankard of froth from his manhood.
Strong as wet ropes, he strode round its warmth.

He gave her an earthenware jug for her cleansing,
took – from her morning-cheek – crumbs of cold sleep,
slops of small tears.

THE ANGEL

And I came to a pool, soul-deep in September;
it lay like a cat in the lap of the land.
And an angel arose like a vase, like a lantern;
his eyes were the lamps of the tame gray tides.

He offered me drink: I preferred to be thirsty,
to hear the terse words of a waterless noon.
He offered me silks: I sought to stay ugly in tatters of tensions.
He offered me shelter, his lean arms extending the gentlest of gospels.
He offered me healing: my memories wept like an army of lamed ones.
He stepped forward, as if to lift me from their weeping.

Too late. I had chosen the aggression, the known bear of north wind –
whose deadliest glory I thought to be godly.
The autumn sun kept my guilt warm; the wind aired it,
took it for walks on a long leash of scoldings,
made of my angel a crumble of leaves, an hallucination.

The pool remained feline, tolerant, placid:
it awaited my sorrow.

THE COLD AND THE WARM

The first pain of cold
is the lake wrinkling dry on the winter-bent back,
the apple core wedged between front teeth of thought,
the sliver of stained glass disrupting the dream.

The second pain of cold
is the thickening of feelings, the carelessly lumpy,
the blunder of muscles, the nearly-not-born,
the blunt voice. The beast.

The third pain of cold
is the end of the shudder,
the first of the shutters unfolding to sun,
the torch on the eyes grown accustomed to grimness.

See now the thistle-brave wrist
that unties this loose knot of a poem
so deftly!

A YEAR OF DREAMS

I gave my dear an hour of frosts,
my hair untimely white with fear,
my eyes opaque with cold.

I gave my dear a day of flames,
my once numbed fingers stroked to life,
my sore throat spread with sun.

I gave my dear a week of storms:
tempers twisted me limb by limb;
they teased and they tousled my mind.

I gave my dear a month's retreat,
my tranquil cell grown frail with grief,
my silence bright with pain.

I gave my dear a year of dreams
in ships of sleep no storm could wreck,
no frost, no flame, could harm.

A LITTLE SADNESS

**The little demon of my sadness is dipped in an ocean of learning.
I am deliriously young, yet decrepit from fretting.
You permit me to be passive,
to be plucked like a tightly strung lute, but subtly.**

**I cling to your coattails, to the lapels of your confidence;
I hang in your hammock,
I who am a second hand half-light,
a creature of dappled days, of cloudy country.
Here, perhaps, the little sadness may revisit me with its peculiar lotions.
Here – like one twice born – I may bring into focus my buried first world,
through the lens of your strength find compassion for its weakness.**

THE TRESPASSERS

They came in my sleep;
they came with a table, with wolves, with a child;
they scattered their crusts on my sterilised cloth.
The child was unwell;
and I watched how the wolves were his will, were his walls.

"Touch me," he cried.
"I will trespass no longer when healed!"
His desolate voice was a catkin of light,
a chime in my paralysis.
It was I who was touched.

THE FAMILY

Brother Fire strikes first:
he dries up the smile on the lips, in the eyes;
he dries up the tears on the lids, in the lungs;
purple with speed, he peels off my pride.

Sister Rain spits at him:
she promises paintings of pity on pain;
she smoothes over selfhood with pastes of deception;
foolishly she wallows in her wetness.

Child Wind follows loudly:
his haunts are my hollows;
he puffs at the rain, at the relics of ash;
he pecks at my tongue with his northernmost beak.

Estranged, they are ravens: together they are Dove.
For the beauty of Fire is his nursery of light,
and the beauty of Rain is her wing of white cloud,
and the beauty of Wind is his soundness of breath.

THE REJECTED

"I would bring you a birthday, a candle of sound,
a round house of nouns, a pavement of verbs,"
persuades Mind.

"Now is not the time,"
say the feelings – like beasts in their womb-warm hay.

"See here," pleads Mind,
"a wardrobe of words, a cathedral of phrases!"

"Now is not the time," say the feelings.
"But when we are big, we shall send you our herald –
a blind child, afraid of the size of its heart.
Now is not the time
for the breakdown of dams,
for the firmaments of terror,
for the pre-world void."

Mind, with its words, leaves emptily, sadly,
eyes puzzled cold as the moon.

THE INFANT

I had worn my best buds for the brides of Easter,
my tabards of leaves for the Pentecost birds;
I had kissed with my last fruit the Michaelmas children.

They mocked,
"You are old, too old for our love."

I stood like a mourner, stood sleeping in dead grass,
a hole in my heart.

The giant Winter loped towards me,
carried on an eyelash the infant Spring;
he pierced through my wood with his spear of a thumbnail.

The infant felt cold, too cold for complaint.
And I saw that his hair had the fairness of brides,
that his shawl was of leaves,
that the orb of the world, which he held in his hands, was my
Michaelmas fruit.

THE OLD AND THE NEW

That *Old* Year, gray as the rutted snow,
is sore with loss, reluctant to go
where bleak seas roar.

Like firstborn leaves on the stiles of spring,
this *New* Year beckons, coldly bright;
her finger is polished with sweets of dew;
her lip shows mauve, like a storm-struck light.

"Come!" she commands, in a voice so pure
that the gray one winces, blackens and breaks,
is deafened by fright.

FINALE

I remember the music –
the fanfare of March with its frail yellow trumpets,
the descant of rainbows,
the full choir of sun,
the soloist ceasing, exultant as belfries.

I remember the Christmas concealed in its furs,
the ribbons of Easter, the buttress of birthdays,
the comfort of customs, the challenge of change,
the pressed flower, which indicates the novelty of solitude,
the plain face of home.